Howard Willoughby

Australian Pictures

Drawn from pen and pencil

Howard Willoughby

Australian Pictures
Drawn from pen and pencil

ISBN/EAN: 9783337312640

Printed in Europe, USA, Canada, Australia, Japan

Cover: Foto ©Thomas Meinert / pixelio.de

More available books at **www.hansebooks.com**

Australian Pictures

Drawn with Pen and Pencil

BY

HOWARD WILLOUGHBY
OF 'THE MELBOURNE ARGUS

*WITH A MAP AND ONE HUNDRED AND SEVEN ILLUSTRATIONS FROM SKETCHES
AND PHOTOGRAPHS, ENGRAVED BY E. WHYMPER AND OTHERS.*

LONDON
THE RELIGIOUS TRACT SOCIETY
56 PATERNOSTER ROW AND 164 PICCADILLY
1886

LONDON:
PRINTED BY WILLIAM CLOWES AND SONS, Limited,
STAMFORD STREET AND CHARING CROSS.

IN THE MOUNTAINS, FERNSHAW.

PREFACE.

IN one respect this work differs from its predecessors. The companion volumes were written by travellers to the lands which they described, but AUSTRALIAN PICTURES are by an Australian resident. Hence, when praise is required, the author has often preferred to quote some traveller of repute rather than to state his own impressions. Thanks have to be given to the Government of Victoria, which kindly placed all its works at the disposal of the author. The official history of the aborigines compiled by Mr. Brough Smyth is especially a valuable storehouse of facts for future writers. The proprietors of the *Melbourne Argus* liberally gave the use of the views and pictures of their illustrated paper, the *Australian Sketcher*, and the offer was gratefully and largely taken advantage of. Mr. R. Wallen, a President of the Art Union of Victoria, gave permission for the reproduction of any of the works of art published by the society during his term of office. Australia is a large place, and it will be seen that, where the author could not refresh his memory by a personal visit, he has here and there availed himself of the willing aid of literary friends.

THE SCOTS' CHURCH, COLLINS STREET, MELBOURNE.

CONTENTS.

Mount Kosciusko . . . . *Frontispiece*
In the Mountains, Fernshaw 5
The Scots' Church, Collins Street, Melbourne . . . 6

Section I.—Introductory.

CHAPTER I.
INTRODUCTION.

AREA OF AUSTRALIA—ENGLAND'S HERITAGE—NATURAL RICHES—POPULATION—PRESENT PROSPECTS OF IMMIGRANTS—THE SIX COLONIES—FACILITIES OF TRAVEL—CHARACTER OF PEOPLE. *pages* 11-16

Illustrations:

A Native Climbing a Tree for Opossum . . *page* 12   A Road through an Australian Forest . . *page* 13
Coranderrk Station 16

CHAPTER II.
CONFIGURATION AND CLIMATE.

DIMENSIONS OF AUSTRALIA—MOUNT KOSCIUSKO—THE MURRAY RIVER SYSTEM—WIND LAWS—THE HOT WIND—INTENSE HEAT PERIODS—THE EARLY EXPLORERS—STURT'S EXPERIENCE—BLACKS AND BUSH FIRES—DROUGHTS—UNEXPLORED AUSTRALIA. *pages* 17-26

Illustrations:

The Giant Gum-tree . . . . . . *page* 18   Junction of Murray and Darling Rivers . . *page* 20
Railroad through the Gippsland Forest . . 19   The National Museum, Melbourne . . . 26

CHAPTER III.
THE AUSTRALIAN PEOPLE.

AUSTRALIAN DEMOCRACIES—THE FEDERAL MOVEMENT—IMMIGRATION—CURRENT WAGES—COST OF LIVING—ABSENCE OF AN ESTABLISHED CHURCH—RELIGION IN THE RURAL DISTRICTS—A TYPICAL SERVICE—SUNDAY OBSERVANCE—MISSION WORK—CHURCH BUILDING. *pages* 27-34

Illustrations:

Statue of Prince Albert in Sydney . . *page* 28   The Bower-Bird . . . *page* 29
The Independent Church, Collins Street, Melbourne . . 33

Section II.—Bird's-eye View of the Colonies.

CHAPTER IV.

VICTORIA.

PORT PHILLIP—EARLY SETTLEMENT AND ABANDONMENT—THE PIONEERS HENTY, BATMAN AND FAWKNER —SIZE OF VICTORIA—MELBOURNE—ITS APPEARANCE—PUBLIC BUILDINGS—STREETS—RESERVES—PRIDE OF ITS PEOPLE—UNEARNED INCREMENT—SANDHURST—BALLARAT—THE CAPITAL OF THE INTERIOR — GEELONG — THE WESTERN DISTRICT — VIEW OF THE LAKES — PORTLAND — THE WHEAT PLAINS — SHEPPERTON—THE MALLEE—GIPPSLAND—MOUNTAIN RANGES—SCHOOL SYSTEM—COLE'S COACHES—FACTS AND FIGURES.

Illustrations:
Page 35-72

Semi-Civilised Victorian Aborigines	Page 36	The Fitzroy Gardens, Melbourne	Page 53
Government House, Melbourne	37	The Yarra Yarra, near Melbourne	55
Melbourne, 1840	40	Bird's-eye View of Sandhurst	58
A Railway Pier in Melbourne in 1886	41	On Lake Wellington	63
A Melbourne Suburban House	44	A Victorian Lake	65
Bird's-eye View of Melbourne showing Public Offices	46	The Upper Goulbourn, Victoria	66
Bird's-eye View of Melbourne looking Southwards	47	Waterfall in the Black Spur	68
Bird's-eye View of Central Melbourne	50	A Victorian Forest	69
Bourke Street, Melbourne, looking East	51	Staging Scenes	71
University, Melbourne	52	A Sharp Corner	72

CHAPTER V.

NEW SOUTH WALES.

SURVEY OF THE COLONY—SYDNEY AND ITS HARBOUR—THE GREAT WEST—THE BLUE MOUNTAINS—THEIR GRAND SCENERY—AN AUSTRALIAN SHOW PLACE—THE FISH RIVER CAVES — DUBBO TO THE DARLING— THE GREAT PASTURES—THE NORTHERN TABLELAND—THE BIG SCRUB COUNTRY—TROPICAL VEGETATION.

Page 73-96

Views in Sydney: Government House, the Cathedral, and Sydney Heads	Page 74	Macquarie Street, Sydney	Page 83
		The Town Hall, Sydney	85
Government Buildings, Macquarie Street, Sydney	75	Emu Plains	88
Statue of Captain Cook at Sydney	77	The Valley of the Grose	89
The Post Office, George Street, Sydney	80	Zigzag Railway in the Blue Mountains	91
Sydney Harbour	82	Fish River Caves	92
Waterfall at Gowett			93

CHAPTER VI.

SOUTH AUSTRALIA.

CONFIGURATION—THE LAKE COUNTRY—HEAT IN SUMMER—FRUIT—GLENELG—ADELAIDE—MOUNT LOFTY RANGE—PARKS AND BUILDINGS—MOSQUITO PLAIN CAVES—CAMELS—THE OVERLAND TELEGRAPH LINE— PEAKE STATION—THE NORTHERN TERRITORY—EARLY MISFORTUNES—PRESENT PROSPECTS—INSECT LIFE —ALLIGATORS—BUFFALOES.

Illustrations:
Page 97-114

Overland Telegraph Party	Page 98	An Adelaide Public School	Page 105
Government House and General Post Office, Adelaide	99	Reaping in South Adelaide	106
Waterfall Gully, South Australia	100	Camel Scenes	108
A Murray River Boat	101	Peake Overland Telegraph Station	109
Adelaide in 1837	102	Collingrove Station, South Australia	111
King William Street, Adelaide	104	Sheep in the Shade of a Gum-tree	112
The Botanical Gardens, Adelaide			114

CHAPTER VII.

QUEENSLAND.

Size and Configuration—Early Settlement—Brisbane Island and Coast Towns—Gladstone—Roma—Gympie—Toowoomba—Townsville—Cooktown—Squatting—The Cattle Station—The Sheep Station—The Queensland Forest—The Nettle-tree—Sugar Planting—Polynesian Natives—Stoppage of the Labour Trade—Gold Mining—The Palmer—Silver, Tin, and Copper.

pages 115-130

Illustrations:

Brisbane . . . . *page* 116	Valley of the River Brisbane, Queensland . *page* 120
A Village on Darling Downs 117	Townsville, North Queensland 124
Sugar Plantation, Queensland	 127

CHAPTER VIII.

WESTERN AUSTRALIA.

Early Settlement—Mistaken Land System—Convict Labour—The System Abandoned—Poison Plants—Perth—King George's Sound—Climate—Pearls—Prospects. *pages* 131-140

Illustrations:

Sheep-Shearing . . . *page* 132	Government House, Perth . *page* 137
Perth 133	Albany 139

CHAPTER IX.

TASMANIA.

A Holiday Resort for Australians—Launceston—The North and South Esk—Mount Bischoff—A Wild District—The Old Main Road—Hobart—The Derwent—Port Arthur—Convicts—Facts and Figures. *pages* 141-152

Illustrations:

View of Mount Wellington, Tasmania . *page* 142	Views in Tasmania . *page* 147
Corra Lynn, Tasmania 143	Launceston 148
On the South Esk, Tasmania . . . 145	Hell Gate, Tasmania . . . 149
On the River Derwent 152	

Section III.—Australian Life and Products.

CHAPTER X.

HEROES OF EXPLORATION.

Tragic Stories—Flinders and Bass—Adventures in a Small Boat—Discoveries—Disappearance of Bass—Death of Flinders—Eyre's Journey—Ludwig Leichardt—Disappearance of his Party—Theory of his Fate—The Kennedy Catastrophe—The Burke and Wills Expedition—Across the Continent—The Deserted Depôt—Slow Death by Starvation—Later Expeditions. *pages* 153-164

Illustrations:

Native Encampment . . . *page* 154	Splitters in the Forest . *page* 157
A New Clearing 155	After Stray Cattle . . . 160
Monument to Burke and Wills in Melbourne . 163	

CHAPTER XI.

A GLANCE AT THE ABORIGINES.

First Encounter with the Blacks—Misunderstandings—Narrative of a Pioneer—Climbing Trees—The Blacks' Defence—Decay of the Race—Weapons—The Northern Tribes—A Northern Encampment—Corroboree—Black Trackers—Burial—Mission Stations. *pages* 165-178

Illustrations:

A Corroboree	*page* 166	A Native Encampment in Queensland	*page* 174
A Waddy Fight	167	A Native Tracker	175
Civilised Aborigines	169	Church, Schoolhouse, and Encampment at Lake	
A Boomerang	173	Tyers	176

CHAPTER XII.

SOME SPECIMENS OF AUSTRALIAN FAUNA AND FLORA.

Marsupials—The 'Tasmanian Devil'—Dingoes—Kangaroo Hunting—The Lyre-Bird—Bower-Bird—The Giant Kingfisher—Emu Hunting—Snakes—The Shark—Alleged Monotony of Vegetation—Tropical Vegetation of Coast—The Giant Gum—The Rostrata—The Mallee Scrub—Flowers and Shrubs. *pages* 179-202

Illustrations:

Australian Tree-Ferns	*page* 180	The Giant Kingfisher, or Laughing Jackass	*page* 189
Dingoes	181	The Emu	190
The *Sarcophilus* or 'Tasmanian Devil'	182	The Tiger-Snake	192
Bass River Opossum	183	Australian Trees	195
A Kangaroo Battue	184	Silver-stem Eucalypts	198
The Platypus	186	The Bottle-Tree	201
The Lyre-Bird	187	Grass-Trees	202

CHAPTER XIII.

THE SQUATTER AND THE SETTLER.

Present Meaning of the Word 'Squatter'—Cattle-Raising—Capital has Confidence in Squatting Now—Origin of Merino Sheep-Breeding—Management of a Run—Drought—Box-Tree Clearings—Modern Enterprise—Sheep-Shearing—'Sundowners'—Farming Prospects—Cheap Land—Easy Harvesting—Small Capital—Selection Conditions—Bush Fires—Black Thursday—The Otway Disaster—Lost in the Bush—Missing Children. *pages* 203-219

Illustrations:

Droving Cattle	*page* 203	A Bush Welcome	*page* 213
A Merino Sheep	206	Before and After the Fire	216
Ring Barking	209	Found!	218
A Squatter's Station	219		

Appendix . . . 220

Index . . . 221

SECTION I.
INTRODUCTORY.

A Native Climbing a Tree for Opossum

A Road through an Australian Forest.

CHAPTER I.

INTRODUCTORY.

AREA OF AUSTRALIA—ENGLAND'S HERITAGE—NATURAL RICHES—POPULATION—PRESENT PROSPECTS OF IMMIGRANTS—THE SIX COLONIES—FACILITIES OF TRAVEL—CHARACTER OF PEOPLE.

'AUSTRALIAN PICTURES' must necessarily consist of peeps at Australia. It seems presumptuous at first to ask that great island-continent to creep into a single volume. But sketches of parts and bird's-eye views will often reveal more to the stranger than a minute and fatiguing survey of the whole. These pages, though few in number, will, it is hoped, convey to the reader some idea of that vast new world where Saxons and Celts are peacefully building up another Britain.

Some of the early errors about Australia must have already faded away. Few can now believe that her birds are without voice and her flowers without perfume, and that the continent itself is a desert fringed by a habitable seaboard. Yet it is perhaps hardly realised by the many how grand is the heritage secured in Australia for the British race. The extent of territory is enormous. Twenty-five kingdoms the size of Great Britain and Ireland could be carved out of this giant island and its appendages, and still there would be a remainder. Its total area, 2,983,200 square miles, is only a little less than the area of Europe.

At first it was supposed that only a limited portion of this enormous tract would be available for settlement, but this fear is dying out. The central desert, that bugbear of a past generation, has an existence, but man is pushing it farther and farther back. Where the explorer perished through thirst a few years ago we now have the homestead and the township; water is conserved, flocks are fed, the property, if it has to be offered for sale, is described as 'that valuable and well-known squatting block.' The tales that were first told were true enough, but man, as he advances, subdues the country and ameliorates the climate.

Already Australia exports to the markets of the world the finest wheat, the finest wool, and the finest gold. Her produce in these lines commands the highest prices, and no test of superiority could be more conclusive. In two at least of these items the export could be indefinitely increased, and meat and wine can be added to the list. On such articles as these man subsists, and they are produced here with a minimum of expense and effort.

The total population of Australia is 2,800,000. The settlers have drawn about themselves over 1,100,000 horses, 8,000,000 cattle, and 70,000,000 sheep. But three millions of men and tens of millions of creatures fail to occupy; they do little more than dot the corners of the great lone island. In the north-west of the continent there are tracts of country which the white man has not yet penetrated. Tribes still roam there who may have heard of the European stranger, but who have never seen him. Adventurous spirits are now pushing into these distant regions, but there will be pioneering work for many a long term of years, and after the pioneer has had his day the task of settlement begins. Even in Victoria and New South Wales, the most thickly populated of the colonies, there are many fertile hillsides and valleys as yet untrodden by man. The population has sought the plains, where the least expenditure was required to make the earth bring forth its increase. Some of the richest land in both colonies has yet to be appropriated, the settler having neglected it because it has to be cleared. The giant eucalypt of the uplands frightened the colonist away to the lightly timbered, park-like plains; but now, thanks to the extension of the railways, the mountain ash, the red gum, and the blackwood, with their companions, are found to be sources of wealth. Thus, in the old states and in the new territories alike, openings exist for the agriculturist and the grazier as favourable as have ever been offered. More fortunes have been made in Australia within the past ten years than have ever been accumulated before. The labourer has put more money than ever into the savings-bank or the building society. The farmer has more rapidly become a comfortable, well-to-do personage; the grazier or squatter has seen his income swell. The value of city property has increased as if by magic. It may be truly said that the chances and prospects of the new arrival are greater to-day, and are likely to be greater for years to come, than they were even in the feverish flush of the gold era.

Australia is for the present divided into six colonies. As time rolls on we may expect six times this number of states. If some of the larger provinces were at all thickly populated they would be absolutely unmanageable for administrative purposes. The states are named Victoria, New South Wales, South Australia, Queensland, Western Australia and Tasmania. They will be noticed in these pages in turn. Victoria, with an area of 87,000 square miles, has a population of a little more than 1,000,000. Thus it is the most densely peopled of the group. Agriculture, gold mining and wool growing are its prominent industries, and it is the colony in which manufactures are most developed. New South Wales has also a population of 1,000,000, with an area of 309,000 square miles. She is a pastoral colony. Queensland, with an area of 668,000 square miles, has less than 350,000 people, a circumstance that shows how little she has been developed. Her industries are pastoral and gold mining; and in the far north sugar plantations have been established under somewhat unhappy auspices. South Australia has an area of 903,000 square miles, and a population under 350,000. Much of her territory is absolutely unexplored. Her little community is clustered about Adelaide, and has relied so far upon the export of wool, copper and, above all, wheat. Last of the continental states comes Western Australia, the Cinderella of the group. Her population is only 35,000, her area is no less than 975,000 square miles, much of it being absolutely unknown, while the greater part has no other occupants than the black man, the emu and the marsupial. Tasmania, the little island colony, has a population of 135,000, and an area of 26,000 square miles.

All the capitals are on the seaboard, and, setting the Western Australian Perth aside, the traveller can proceed from one to the other either by the magnificent liners of the Peninsular and Oriental, the Orient, and the British India Steam Navigation Companies, or he can avail himself of splendid Clyde-built steamers run by local enterprise. Very shortly he will be able to land at either Adelaide or Brisbane, and journey from the one point to the other by rail, as the iron chain is almost continuous now, and missing links are being rapidly completed. Whichever capital he lands at, he will find a network of railways branching into the interior, and seated behind the locomotive he can visit places where a few years back the explorers perished! Only if he is very ambitious of sight-seeing need he have recourse to coach, horse, or the popular American—but acclimatised—buggy.

So far as the people are concerned, he will find that he is still in the old country. Traveller after traveller, Mr. Archibald Forbes and Lord Rosebery in turn, and a host of others, affirm that the typical Australian is apt to be more English than the Englishman. There is no aristocracy, it is true, and no National Church. Each state is a democracy pure and simple, under the English flag. But the Queen has nowhere more devoted and loyal subjects, and nowhere are the Churches more numerous, more active, and apparently more blessed in results. The traveller meets with English manners, English sympathies, and a frank hospitality which, the compilers of books and the deliverers of lectures affirm, is peculiar to Australia. But he finds the race amid novel surroundings, amid scenery whose peculiarity is vastness, with a distinctive vegetation unlike any other, with seasons which have little resemblance to those of the old country; and the occupations of the people, he discovers, are also often new. When a writer undertakes to sketch the scene, it must be his fault if he has nothing of interest to relate.

COORANDERRK STATION.

CONFIGURATION AND CLIMATE.

THE GIANT GUM-TREE.

RAILROAD THROUGH THE GIPPSLAND FOREST.

CHAPTER II.

CONFIGURATION AND CLIMATE.

DIMENSIONS OF AUSTRALIA — MOUNT KOSCIUSKO — THE MURRAY RIVER SYSTEM — WIND LAWS — THE HOT WIND — INTENSE HEAT PERIODS — THE EARLY EXPLORERS — STURT'S EXPERIENCE — BLACKS AND BUSH FIRES — DROUGHTS — UNEXPLORED AUSTRALIA.

IT is not possible to understand Australia without a glance at the physical conditions of the continent. A good angel and a bad, an evil influence and a beneficial, are ever in contention in nature here. From the surrounding sea come cool and grateful clouds; from the heated interior come hot blasts, licking up life and absorbing the watery vapours which would otherwise fall as rain. Sea and land are ever in conflict.

Australia measures from north to south 1700 miles, and from east to west 2400 miles—the total area being somewhat greater than that of the United States of America, and somewhat less than the whole of Europe.

The peculiarity is that all its mountain ranges worth taking notice of—all that are factors in the climate—are comparatively near the coast. Thus the main dip is rather inland than outward, and this formation is fatal to great rivers. An interior mountain chain such as the New Zealand Alps would have transformed the country. The enormous coast-line from Spencer's Gulf to King George's Sound is not broken by the mouth of any stream. Such rainfall as there is in this district must drain either into the sea by subterranean channels, or into the inland marshy depressions called Lake Eyre, Lake Gairdner, and Lake Amadeus, which are sometimes extremely shallow

JUNCTION OF MURRAY AND DARLING RIVERS.

sheets of water, sometimes grassy plains, and sometimes desert. The best land is that between the various ranges and the sea, because there most rain falls. And the greatest of the ranges is that which runs from north to south along the east coast of the island, passing through Queensland, New South Wales, and Victoria, and culminating in Mount Kosciusko, whose peak is 7120 feet high, and whose ravines always contain snow. Only at Kosciusko does snow lie all the year round in Australia, though the mountains near it, about 6000 feet high, are also almost always covered. To this range we owe the one river system at all worthy of the continent.

The waters from the western side of the Queensland mountains—there called the Dividing Range—flow down the Warrego into the Darling. Here they are joined by the waters from the higher ranges of New South Wales and Victoria, called the Australian Alps. These waters have been brought down by the Murray, the Murrumbidgee, and the Goulburn, and the united floods fall into the sea, through Lake Alexandrina, between Melbourne and Adelaide.

On paper this river system shows well. The Darling has been navigated up to Walgett, which is 2345 miles from the sea, and this distance entitles the Australian stream to rank third among the rivers of the world, only the Mississippi and the Amazon coming before it. But the facts are not so good as they seem. The Darling depends upon flood waters. Sometimes these flood waters will come down in sufficient volume to enable the stream to run from end to end, and sometimes they fail half-way. The river is never open to navigation all the year round, and frequently it is not open to navigation from year's end to year's end. The occasional failure of the Darling for so long a period upsets all calculations. The colonists will take this stream and the river Murray in hand some day, and will lock both and preserve their storm waters, and the south-eastern corner of the continent will then have a grand river communication. Stores will then be sent up, and wool will be brought down with certainty, where now all is doubt and speculation. Commissions to consider the subject have been appointed both by the Victorian Government and the Government of New South Wales, and conferences are this year (1886) being held upon it and cognate subjects. Unhappily, there are no other streams in Australia that can be so dealt with, though it should be added that the last has not yet been heard of the rivers of Northern Australia. We are ignorant of their capacities, though a good guess can be made about them.

Taking Australia from east to west, we find a high range skirting the coast on the east, and supporting a dense sub-tropical vegetation, and giving rise to an extensive but uncertain river system. Next comes a more sterile interior, composed of desert, of shallow salt lakes, and of higher steppes in unknown proportions. Approaching the west coast we meet ranges again, and rivers and fertile country.

Mr. H. C. Russell, Government Astronomer for New South Wales, in his valuable pamphlet on the 'Physical Geography and Climate of New South Wales,' points out that 'if water flowed over the whole of the Australian continent, the trade wind would then blow steadily over the northern portions from the south-east, and above it the like steady return current would blow to the south-east, while the "brave west winds" and southerly would hold sway over the other half—conditions which now exist a short distance from the coast. Into this system Australia introduces an enormous disturbing element, of which the great interior plains form the most active agency in changing the directions of the wind currents. The interior, almost treeless and waterless, acts in summer like a great oven with more than tropical heating power, and becomes the great motor force on our winds, by causing an uprush, and consequent inrush on all sides, especially on the north-west, where it has power sufficient to draw the north-east trade over the equator, and into a north-west monsoon, in this way wholly obliterating the south-east trade belonging to the region, and bringing the monsoon with full force on to Australia, where, being warmed, and receiving fresh masses of heated air, it rises and forms part of the great return current from the equator to the south.'

The 'hot winds' of the colonists are produced by the sinking down to the surface of the heated current of air, which in summer is continually passing overhead; and when this wind blows in force upon a clear summer's day things are not pleasant. The thermometer from time to time indicates a degree of heat which is almost incredible. In Southern Melbourne the official record gives a reading of 179 degrees in the sun, and 111 in the shade, and at the inland town of Deniliquin, the official register in the shade is 121 degrees. Man and beast and vegetation suffer on these days. The birds drop dead from the trees, the fruit is scorched and rendered unfit for market. The leaves of the English trees, such as the plane and the elm, drop in profusion, so that in early summer it will seem as if autumn had set in. The sick, especially children, are terribly affected, and the doctors attending an infant sufferer will say that nothing can be done except to pray for a change of wind. Happily, such days as these are rare. The hot blast will not often send the temperature up to more than 100 to 105 degrees, and the duration of the heated wind is limited to three days, and often it prevails during only one, sunset bringing with it a cool southern gale.

A moderate hot wind is relished by many people, for the air is dry and even exhilarating to the strong for a while; and the claim is made that it destroys noxious germs and effluvia. Sometimes the hot wind will gradually die out, but on other occasions a rushing storm will come up from the south, driving the north wind before it, and in that case the welcome conflict will be preceded by whirling and blinding clouds of dust, and will be accompanied by thunder and lightning and torrents of rain. The fall of the temperature will be something marvellous. The thermometer will be standing at 150° in the sun; then the wind will change, rain will fall, and in the evening the register will be 50°, making a difference of 100 degrees in seven or eight hours.

That these days are exceptional is shown by the manner in which vegetation generally flourishes, and by the admiration which each colonist has for the climate of that particular part of Australia in which he resides. 'The Swan Settlements,' says the Western Australian, 'are the pick of the country. No hot winds there.' At Adelaide the visitor is told: 'Yes, we are often hotter by ten degrees in the sun than they are in Melbourne, but ours is a dry, not a moist heat.' In Melbourne the tale is reversed: 'Sydney is muggy,' it is averred; 'you cannot stand that. A dry heat is the thing, but those poor beggars at Adelaide have it too hot altogether.'

No doubt many mistakes occurred in the descriptions of Australia given by the early explorers. Brave and intelligent as they were, they were 'new chums,' and certainly not born bushmen. Transplanted from a small island, continental features overpowered them. Forests which took weeks to traverse; plains, like the ocean, horizon-bounded; the vast length of our rivers when compared to those of England, often flowing immense distances without change or tributary—now all but dry for hundreds of miles, at other times flooding the countries on their banks to the extent of inland seas—wearied them. Then we know that our cloudless skies, the mirage, the long-sustained high range of the thermometer in the central portion of the continent, troubled them a good deal more than they do us, and helped to make them look on the dark side of things. Hence, as a rule, their reports were unfavourable.

Sturt's account of his detention at Depôt Glen is enough to frighten anybody, and cannot be read to this day without emotion. Here, 'stuck up' by want of water, he dug an underground room, and he and his men passed a terrible summer. The heat was sometimes as high as 130 degrees in the shade, and in the sun it was altogether intolerable. They were unable to write, as the ink dried at once on their pens; their combs split; their nails became brittle and readily broke; and if they touched a piece of metal it blistered their fingers. Month after month passed without a shower of rain. Sometimes they watched the clouds gather, and they could hear the distant roll of thunder, but there fell not a drop to refresh the dry and dusty desert. The party began to grow thin and weak; Mr. Poole, the second in command, became ill with scurvy. At length, when the winter was approaching, a gentle shower moistened the plain; and preparations were being made to send the sick man quickly to the Darling, when Poole died, and the mournful cavalcade returned, leaving a grave in the wilderness. Yet this locality proved in time to be a very good sheep-run, differing in nothing from others around it; and eventually was found to be a gold-field, and was extensively worked. Runs about the spot are commonly advertised in the Melbourne or Sydney papers as carrying immense flocks, and as valued with the stock at from £50,000 to £100,000. The explorer was, in fact, within a few miles of Cooper's Creek.

This process of conquering the interior is still going on. Man modifies all countries, and Australia is no exception to the rule. Even the blacks played their part, and it was a mischievous one. They had an instrument in their hands by which they influenced the whole course of nature. This was the fire-stick. With this implement the aborigines were constantly setting fire to the grass and trees, both accidentally and systematically, for hunting purposes, and probably in their day almost every part of New Holland was swept over by a fierce fire on an average once in five years. Hence the baked, calcined condition of the ground in many parts of the continent, the character of our vegetation, and the comparative scarcity of animal life. The eucalypts survived the fiery ordeal, because of the hardness of their bark; and, when every other creature perished, or had to abandon its litter, the marsupials leaped over the flames with their young in their pouches. Strange as the assertion may appear in the first instance, it may be doubted whether any section of the human race has exercised a greater influence on the physical condition of a large portion of the globe than the wandering savages of Australia. The white man is working in an entirely opposite direction. By clearing the forest he limits the area of the bush fire. He constructs reservoirs, dams rivers, sinks wells in order to bring subterranean water to the surface, and irrigates land, so that a spot where even the hardiest scrub failed to grow in its natural state, is covered with luxuriant crops. Province after province has been rescued from the wilderness already, and the grand work is likely to go on. Those who look at what has been done in the way of reclaiming territory in Australia will be in no hurry to set bounds as to what man is likely to perform.

It is not wonderful that the first inquiry of the practical settler should be as to the rainfall of the country he proposes to occupy. The map most eagerly scanned in Australia is the 'rainfall' map, prepared by the Government, and issued by the leading weekly papers. A glance at this production reveals the tale which it tells. The coast-line is shown in a dark blue, to indicate the heavy rainfall of from thirty to seventy inches. A pleasant blue represents a moderate rainfall on the interior belt of plains, averaging from fifteen to twenty-five inches. Then comes a faint tint spread over what is called the 'never, never' country, where the rainfall is five or ten inches per annum, and where the rain will descend at once, or for two years there will be none, and then the whole average supply will drop from the clouds in one rushing downpour. Under such circumstances it will be readily imagined that the terror of the Australian settler is a drought. Even in the moments of his utmost prosperity he has his anxieties about the next season. A district which has been rainless for a year or two years is a pitiful spectacle of desolation. The grass disappears; the wind carries with it whirling columns of dust; the trees of the dreary plain become more sombre and mournful than ever. If there is a little water left in any dam or reservoir, it is rendered putrid by the carcases of sheep and cattle, for the wretched animals become so weak that, once they fall or stick, they are unable to rise or to extricate themselves. The sun rises in heat, sails through a cloudless sky, and sets a ball of fire. The nights are dewless. The moon only renders more ghastly the depressing panorama.

Mr. Russell complains that pictures of the drought are usually exaggerated, and it may be well therefore to quote official figures. In two years, according to Mr. Dibbs, Treasurer and Premier of New South Wales (November 1885), the drought in New South Wales has killed 200,000 horses, 1,500,000 head of cattle, and 13,500,000 sheep. A loss which is estimated at from £10,000,000 to £15,000,000 has fallen upon a single colony, and a single industry in that colony! But this drought was felt with equal severity in parts of South Australia and of Queensland, and it would be no exaggeration therefore to double the figures communicated to Parliament by Mr. Dibbs. And when 400,000 horses, 3,000,000 cattle, and 27,000,000 sheep die miserably of hunger and thirst, it is certain that scenes must occur the gloom and wretchedness of which can hardly be overpainted. One squatting company in the north lost 150,000 sheep out of 250,000 in the drought in question, and the survivors were kept alive with difficulty. Scrub was cut down for them. The living gnawed the bones of the dead. The company's shares went down to two shillings in the pound, and other squatting property similarly situated was equally depreciated, when one January morning, 1886, the Melbourne, Sydney, Brisbane, and Adelaide papers gave prominence to the welcome news of the break-up of the drought. From this place, that place, and the other, all down the line, came telegrams of the fall of three inches, four inches, five inches, and six inches of rain, the water saturating the ground, filling the dams, and sending the price of pastoral property up as though by magic.

The drought disaster, of course, is most felt in the newly taken-up country. Here a state of nature obtains, while, as time rolls on, and profits are made, water is conserved, and the run is practically made drought-proof. A minimum quantity of stock can be kept, and the remainder can be travelled to a district which is not smitten. The recuperative powers of the country are enormous; and if the squatter is afflicted one year he holds on, with the consciousness that with three or four good seasons in succession he is a made man.

How little we yet know of Australia as a whole has been brought under the popular notice by an address delivered by Mr. Ernest Favenc at a meeting of the Australian Geographical Society, held at Sydney in January 1886. South Australia alone has an area of 250,000 square miles unexplored, and Western Australia has an enormous tract of 500,000 square miles, which has been just rushed through, and no more, by three explorers, Messrs. Forrest, Giles, and Warburton. Here is a total of unknown area equivalent to the heart of Europe—say to Germany, France, Switzerland, Austria, and Hungary, with Italy thrown in. Of course the country to the west of the Overland Telegraph Line, being for the most part unknown, is all described as hopeless desert, but Mr. Favenc doubts the story, and no one is better qualified to express an opinion upon the subject than this gentleman. He stands in the first rank of practical pioneers. The facts that go to support the idea of the existence of large belts of rich prairie land in this huge area are these: In the far interior the transition from barren desert country to rolling downs is sudden and abrupt; without warning, you step from one to the other. The good and the bad country lie very much in bands; and an explorer making an easterly and westerly track might travel in a bad band continuously, if he had the misfortune to strike one.

Mr. Favenc's suggestion is that a well-supplied party should start from a station on the Overland Telegraph Line, and should strike for Perth, making, however, extensive excursions on both sides of their route. The bee-line business is almost useless. It would be well if the Australian Geographical Society could take up the idea, for it is somewhat of a reproach to the three millions of inhabitants that Australia should be less mapped out than Africa; and there is pleasure also in reducing to its narrowest limits that bugbear of the youth of the colonies, the great fiery untamed Central Desert.

If, however, no more exploration be resolved upon, the work will only be postponed, and not abandoned. As one coral insect builds over the other, or as one wave on a rising tide overlaps its predecessor on the shore, so the last outlying pastoral station is speedily passed by one just beyond it. In this way settlement creeps on. Progress, though slow and unsensational, is sure.

THE NATIONAL MUSEUM, MELBOURNE.

THE AUSTRALIAN PEOPLE.

STATUE OF PRINCE ALBERT IN SYDNEY.

THE BOWER-BIRD.

CHAPTER III.

THE AUSTRALIAN PEOPLE.

AUSTRALIAN DEMOCRACIES—THE FEDERAL MOVEMENT—IMMIGRATION—CURRENT WAGES—COST OF LIVING—ABSENCE OF AN ESTABLISHED CHURCH—RELIGION IN THE RURAL DISTRICTS—A TYPICAL SERVICE—SUNDAY OBSERVANCE—MISSION WORK—CHURCH BUILDING.

THE Australian colonies are, one and all, democracies of the most advanced type. Annual Parliaments have been advocated, though at present triennial legislatures are the rule. Payment of members, it should be added, is not adopted by all the states, but the principle seems to be spreading. Two Houses are established in each colony, a Legislative Assembly and a Legislative Council. The former is always elected by manhood suffrage; the latter, as in Victoria and South Australia, may be an elected body, or, as in New South Wales and Queensland, it may be composed of members nominated by the Crown. How the second chamber should be constituted is one of the problems of the day. Every now and then one or the other of the colonies is treated to 'a deadlock' between the two bodies; and more than once in Victoria public payments have been suspended in consequence, and popular passion has run high.

The Australian democracy has worked well upon the whole, and has given security to life and property. The best proof of this is the rapid rise of colonial securities in the public favour. When New South Wales, South Australia, and Victoria commenced to build their national railways in 1857-1860, they were glad to sell six per cent. debentures at par in London, and now they float four per cent. loans at a premium.

The colony of Victoria is altogether protectionist, and South Australia has given in a partial adherence to the system. To the author the policy seems to be wrong in theory and practice, but the belief is widespread that, even if sacrifices are made, the resources of the colony are thus developed.

Twenty years back the populations of the various colonies did not touch each other: each colony spread from its own centre; but now this isolation has disappeared. Settlement is contiguous with settlement, and trade and intercourse are accelerated accordingly. The colonies can no longer ignore each other, and hence the movement for federation has gathered strength.

The first Federal Council met in Hobart in January 1886, but unfortunately jealousies had crept in, and the new body was shorn of its fair proportions. Federalists cannot help feeling greatly disappointed that the results hitherto have been so small, and yet probably there is much more to rejoice over than to be downcast about.

Victoria, Queensland, Tasmania and Western Australia were represented at the Council, and such laws as it can pass will thus affect three-fifths of the area of the continent. The absence of South Australia is understood to be accidental. She is really one of the parties to the federal bond, having agreed to the terms, and having invited the Imperial Parliament to pass the Enabling Act, and her early adhesion is expected with confidence. No continental state will then remain outside except New South Wales, and it is fairly to be presumed that she will not be insensible to the pressure of public opinion, both in Australia and throughout the Empire, especially as care is being taken to soothe the local susceptibilities that are now offended. The Federal Council meets for the present at Hobart, the chief town of Tasmania, and this town may, for the present, be called the 'federal capital.'

The immigration into Australia is about eighty thousand men and women yearly. If double or treble that number came, they could well be accommodated. The labourer of to-day is the employer of to-morrow; and as soon as a man acquires landed property his chief complaint is the paucity of hands to improve his holding.

A few specimens of wages may be taken from the official list of Mr. H. H. Hayter, Government Statist of Victoria. On the whole, labour is more in request in Victoria than in most of the sister states, and the figures may be taken as representing fair average rates for Australia generally. Servants, with board, coachmen, and grooms, 20s. to 30s. per week; female cooks, £40 to £65 per annum; laundresses, £35 to £52 per annum; general servants, 10s. to 14s. per week (these figures are for 1884, and there has been a heavy rise in 1885-6); ploughmen, 25s. per week and board; blacksmiths, 10s. to 14s. per day; boiler-makers, 10s. to 14s. per day; plumbers, £3 to £3 10s. per week; lumpers, 10s. to 12s. per day; masons, carpenters, bricklayers and plasterers, 10s. to 12s. per day.

On the other hand, the necessaries of life are cheap. Bread is 6d. the 4lb. loaf, and beef and mutton are retailed at from 3d. to 8d. per lb.; butter varies from 9d. to 1s. 6d. according to the season; milk is 4d. to 6d. per quart; potatoes 2s. 6d. to 4s. per cwt.; tea 1s. 6d. to 2s. 6d. per lb.; rabbits are sold at 1s. per pair, and hares at 2s. each.

In the Australian colonies there is neither an Established Church, nor is any aid given by the State to the cause of religion. The denominations are now entirely dependent upon the voluntary exertions of their members for support. A strong feeling has grown up both among politicians and the people in Australia that the State ought not to interfere in ecclesiastical matters upon any pretext. The Churches, therefore, are simply corporations empowered to hold property upon certain conditions, and at liberty to manage their own affairs as they think fit.

There are, however, great difficulties in the way of maintaining religious services regularly. In many of the country districts the population is sparse and scattered; and, however willing the people may be, the paucity of their numbers renders it hard for them to support a church. Only a mere handful can be gathered together, most of whom have a hard struggle in their private lives; for, although they own the land which they cultivate, they have to wait until it is cleared for the expected return. The difficulty is enhanced by the fact that each denomination wishes to have a footing in every village, in order to meet the wants of its own people. In many townships where there is room for one strong and self-supporting Protestant congregation, there are three or four, each of which is embarrassed by its own weakness. Some attempt has been made to prevent the weaknesses of disunion by co-operation among the Churches. The Episcopalians and the Presbyterians combine to support a society which is intended to supply the religious wants of the rural population. The money that is thus raised is spent principally in the erection of buildings, which are used alternately by clergymen of each denomination, so that the preferences of the people for their own form of service are gratified at the least cost, and without any rivalry.

By such means the Churches have spread their network well over the land. There is not a township of any importance that cannot boast of two or three neat and substantial edifices dedicated to the service of God. There is not a district that is not visited at intervals by ministers or agents of the different denominations, some of whom have to ride long distances in order to overtake every part. The vast plains that stretch between the rivers Darling and Murray are traversed by clergymen who visit from station to station. The deep forests of Gippsland and the Otway ranges, inhabited by a hardy race of farmers whose lives are spent in clearing the jungle, are not left unprovided for. Though everything is not done that could be desired, it may be said with perfect truth that the Churches strive earnestly to keep pace with the continual migration of the people towards the backwoods of the country.

It is a pleasant thing to attend a rural service on a typical Australian day, when the sun is hot and the sky cloudless, and the whole landscape steeped in peace and quiet. Driving along the road, we see the sheep couched in the grass, or we pass a clearing where wheat and oats are growing among the blackened stumps of fallen trees; and nothing disturbs the stillness of the scene save, perhaps, the lazy motion of a crow, or the rush of a startled native bear, a sleepy, gentle, little animal, an enlarged edition of the opossum. The church stands a little apart from the few houses that form the infant township. It is generally built of wood, and surrounded by tall gum-trees, which, however, afford a very scanty shade from the burning heat. Here is gathered on the Sunday morning a collection of buggies and horses, for the people come long distances, and it is necessary in Australia to drive or ride. The congregation stand in groups before the door, chatting over the week's news, and waiting for the clergyman to arrive. The Day of Rest is the only day in the week in which they have an opportunity of meeting, and many come early and loiter with their neighbours till the service begins. They are all browned and tanned by scorching suns, but they speak with the self-same accent that they learnt at home. There are Scotchmen of whom, to judge by their speech and appearance, it is hard to believe that they have not very recently left their native glens, and Irishmen whose brogue is wholly uncorrupted by change of climate. Most of them, however, have been settled for many years on the land, retaining their old customs in the solitude of the bush, and among the rest a due regard for the worship of God. The children have caught, to some extent, the tone of their parents, and one could almost imagine oneself in a remote parish of Britain. The service itself heightens the illusion. The hymn-tunes are old and familiar, and sung very slowly to the accompaniment of a harmonium. The exhortation of the preacher is brief, telling the old and yet ever new story of the Saviour's love, and it is listened to with evident attention. One hour suffices for the whole worship, and the audience contentedly disperse, and turn their faces towards their lonely homes.

In the towns the organisation of the different Churches is effective. Their agencies are at work in the poorer quarters of the large cities, where the evils that exist in the Old World are showing themselves on a smaller scale. They have stood out strenuously for the observance of the Lord's Day, and with marked success. Sunday observance, if not so strict as it is in Scotland, is more general than in England. There is no postal delivery,

Trains are not run on the main lines, and a limited suburban traffic is alone allowed. All movements for restricting labour on the Sunday meet with cordial sympathy and practical support.

Though now independent in their government of the Churches in England

THE INDEPENDENT CHURCH, COLLINS STREET, MELBOURNE.

by which they were originally founded, and which they continue to represent, the colonial Churches maintain a close relationship with the mother-country. Bishops, and the best preachers, are still brought from home to the colonies. All the important congregations send to England for a minister when there happens to be a vacancy, and all the men who have made a deep impression on the community have been trained there. The whole religious and spiritual life of the colonies is inspired and stimulated by that of England, both in the sense that they naturally lean upon the stronger thought of English writers, and that they are guided by ministers who have studied in British universities. There are colleges connected with the more important denominations, which, it is hoped, will gradually grow till they rival those of other lands. As yet they are incompletely equipped, and one or two men have to bear the brunt of work that is usually divided among four or five.

In a new country, which attracts to itself all sorts and conditions of men, nearly every form of belief is represented. Many of the sects, however, are very small, and may be said to be practically confined to the metropolitan cities. The Catholic Apostolic Church, the Swedenborgians, Lutherans, Moravians, Unitarians, and various bodies of unattached Protestants, are thus limited. The Episcopalians, the Roman Catholics, the Presbyterians and Methodists have by far the largest hold on the people, while Independents and Baptists are fairly numerous and influential. Altogether, the Churches provide accommodation for more than one-half of the people, and the ordinary attendance at their principal weekly service amounts to fully one-third.

Sunday-schools flourish in every part of the country. The total number of children attending them is returned in Victoria as $73\frac{1}{2}$ per cent. of the whole who are at the school age, and the average is not much less in any other colony. When allowance is made for the children who are kept at home by parents that prefer to give their own instruction, and for those in the country who cannot well attend a Sunday-school, it is evident that there are comparatively few who receive no religious education at all.

The love of church building, which every nation has displayed, is by no means wanting among the Australians. In every town the ecclesiastical edifices are the chief features, and in the larger cities some of them are imposing structures. Cathedrals are gradually rising in different places. Even the Churches which are not usually credited with paying much respect to outward appearance are inclined to beautify their buildings.

It would be too much to expect that the denominations could lay aside their differences and unite. But a very kindly feeling exists for the most part between them, whether it be due to their equality, or to the novel circumstances in which they were placed when they began their work. That it may continue and tend to further co-operation is the earnest wish of all.

Statistics, giving the most recent facts about the condition of the various Churches in the colonies, will be found in the Appendix.

SECTION II.

BIRD'S-EYE VIEW OF THE COLONIES.

SEMI-CIVILISED VICTORIAN ABORIGINES.

GOVERNMENT HOUSE, MELBOURNE.

CHAPTER IV.

VICTORIA.

PORT PHILLIP—EARLY SETTLEMENT AND ABANDONMENT—THE PIONEERS HENTY, BATMAN AND FAWKNER—SIZE OF VICTORIA—MELBOURNE—ITS APPEARANCE—PUBLIC BUILDINGS—STREETS—RESERVES—PRIDE OF ITS PEOPLE — UNEARNED INCREMENT — SANDHURST — BALLARAT — THE CAPITAL OF THE INTERIOR — GEELONG — THE WESTERN DISTRICT — VIEW OF THE LAKES — PORTLAND — THE WHEAT PLAINS — SHEPPERTON—THE MALLEE—GIPPSLAND—MOUNTAIN RANGES—SCHOOL SYSTEM—COBB'S COACHES- FACTS AND FIGURES.

I T is strange that Victoria should be one of the youngest of the colonies, for Port Phillip was amongst the places first noticed by the early settlers of the continent. Lieutenant Grant, commanding the little brig *Lady Nelson*, observed the inlet in the year 1800, when *en route* for Sydney. In 1802

Governor King, of New South Wales, dispatched the *Lady Nelson*, under Lieutenant Murray, to explore and report. The account given was most favourable of the extent of the bay, the security of its anchorages, and the beauty and apparent fertility of its shores. The result was that it was decided to establish a convict settlement on the shores of the gulf, and in 1803 Colonel Collins and a party of prisoners, with their guards, landed at the site of the now fashionable seaside resort, which has been called Sorrento at the instance of Sir Charles Gavan Duffy, one of the first landowners there. To the lover of beauty the scene, gazing from Sorrento down Capel Sound, is fair; the blue sea ripples at your feet; the high hills around Dromana, draped with the rich ultramarine blue not to be found outside of Australia, form a charming background on which one can gaze and gaze again. But the prose of the situation for Governor Collins was that he was landed on a well-nigh waterless sand-spit, the most sterile portion of the district, the resort to-day of the admirers of loveliness, but shunned even to-day by the practical settler. The citizen in his Sorrento villa is lulled by the roar of the league-long surf which ever breaks on the rocky ocean beach, scarcely a mile away. But circumstances alter human views, and the historian of the expedition reports that the monotonous booming of the breakers irritated and depressed both soldiers and convicts, and made a miserable company still more wretched. A search was made for water that was not brackish, but the right places were missed, and at last, happily for all concerned, the settlement was abandoned in favour of the Hobart colony. Governor Collins rejoiced to get away from the spot, the soldiers rejoiced, and the convicts also, and posterity will never leave off rejoicing that Victoria was left to be a 'free colony' from its inception.

The bad name given to the Port Phillip district clung to it for nearly a generation. The great central desert was supposed to extend to the sea-coast in this direction; but gradually the real district was discovered by 'overlanders' from New South Wales, and at last, in 1824, Hovell and Hume crossed the Murray river, skirted the Australian Alps, and struck the shores of Port Phillip between Geelong and Melbourne. Later on the Messrs. Henty, crossing from Tasmania, established a whaling-station in Portland Bay, and began cultivation also. So the new land was more and more talked about in the existing settlements, just as the new country in North-western Australia is being talked of in Sydney and Melbourne to-day. Tasmania sent the first batch of colonists, an association, with Mr. John Batman at its head, being formed to take up land there. In one sense Batman did take up land on an enormous scale. He landed in May, 1835. He says in a despatch to the Governor of Tasmania: 'After some time and full explanation, I found eight chiefs amongst them who possessed the whole of the territory near Port Phillip. Three brothers, all of the same name, were the principal chiefs, and two of them, men six feet high, very good-looking; the other not so tall, but stouter. The chiefs were fine men. After explanation of what my object was, I purchased five large tracts of land from them—about 600,000 acres, more or less—and delivered over to them blankets, knives, looking-glasses, tomahawks, beads, scissors, flour, &c., as payment for the land; and also agreed to give them a tribute or rent yearly. The parchment the eight chiefs signed this afternoon, delivering to me some of the soil, each of them, as giving me full possession of the tracts of land.' How the blacks could sign a parchment is somewhat of a mystery. Batman seems to have recognised that a performance of this kind would be laughed at, and so he goes on to describe another signing away which took place. He travelled about with the natives, marking boundary trees.

Batman was a hardy bushman, and acquired great fame in Tasmania by his courage in capturing a notorious convict desperado; but if he imagined that these deeds and purchases would ever be recognised, he was as simple as the blacks themselves. As a matter of fact, no one ever took any notice of them. Within a few weeks after the transaction, the second or Fawkner party of settlers were on the river Yarra, had landed in the gully now called Elizabeth Street, Melbourne, and the future capital had been founded. When the deeds were shown to the new arrivals, they laughed and declined to move on, but proceeded to clear away the site of the city. Batman died from the effects of a severe cold in 1839, and 'Batman's Hill,' where he built his hut, has been cleared away to make room for the great Spencer Street railway station. John Batman would probably have become a rich man had he lived, but his estate was frittered away, and his grandchildren are now working in the mass for their living. Quite recently, a subscription having been organised for the purpose, a suitable monument was placed over the grave of the pioneer in the old Melbourne cemetery. The blacks would certainly have very much liked the terms which Batman made with them to have been respected, for Batman spoke of a yearly rent, and no one afterwards ever dreamed of such a provision.

The rival pioneer was much more fortunate. John Pascoe Fawkner lived to a ripe old age, became a member of the Legislative Council, and 'Fawkner's Park,' a handsome city reserve, perpetuates his name; while his portrait is in the Victorian National Gallery. The last time the author met the shrewd old man was in 1870, when he had stopped his carriage on the Eastern Hill to gaze wistfully at the scene, and was ready to talk with animation about the changes that had passed over it. Those changes had been great indeed. On the whole, the lieutenant of the convoy ship *Calcutta* was not exactly happy in his prophecy, when he wrote as he sailed away: 'The kangaroo now reigns undisturbed lord of the Port Phillip soil, and he is likely to retain his dominion for ages.' Sir Thomas Mitchell was more felicitous when, being commissioned by the Sydney Government to explore and report on the country to the south of the Murray, he wrote back in 1836-7: ' A land more favourable for colonisation could not be found. This is *Australia Felix.*

The surface of this south-eastern corner of Australia is strangely diversified, and hence its charm. Its own south-eastern region is occupied by the Australian Alps. Hundreds of peaks rising from 4000 to 7000 feet in height secure here an abundant rainfall, and in the sheltered gullies a noble vegetation is to be found; then come the uplands sloping down to the Murray plains. And back from the western sea-board stretches the beautiful

MELBOURNE, 1840.
(*From the original sketch by Mr. S. H. Haydon.*)

so-called Western District, composed of open rolling plains studded with lakes, and with the isolated cones of extinct volcanoes. A grand and terrible sight they must have presented when these agents were at work sending forth fire, ashes and water, but, happily for man, their powers have departed long, long ago. Mount Franklin shows no sign of becoming a second Vesuvius, and the volcanic deposit has secured for the west a wonderful luxuriance of growth— such a growth as the grazier dearly loves. The beauty of the eastern district of Victoria is of the kind that delights the artist; the pleasant western

A Railway Pier in Melbourne in 1886.

spectacle is grateful to the banker. The capitalist will build a cottage home in the one, but he will advance money freely on the acres of the other. The gold-fields are the least picturesque of any portion of the Austral region, though as gold-fields they possess a romance of their own.

But, turning from the country to the town, we have first and foremost that special pride of Victoria, the great city of Melbourne. Batman proclaimed the site 'a good spot for a village,' and the village has become a metropolis. We give an engraving showing what Melbourne was like in 1840, and as a contrast, one of a railway pier in the same city forty-six years later. Its population of over 350,000 puts Melbourne into the rank of the first score of the cities of the empire. And if area were considered as the test, the city would not easily be surpassed, except by London itself, for a ten miles' radius from the Post Office is required to cover it all. There is much filling in to be done, of course, but Brighton, Oakleigh, Surrey Hills, and other of the long distance suburbs have not only been built up to, but are being passed by the spreading population. The city itself is a compact mass of about a mile and a half square, encircled by large parks and gardens, all the property of the people, and permanently reserved for their use. Built upon a cluster of small rolling hills, the views of Melbourne are pleasantly interrupted, and yet it is possible to obtain frequent glimpses from commanding points, either of the whole or of parts of the whole. You will turn a corner and come upon a panoramic peep of streets, of sea and of spires that takes one's breath away. Near Bishopscourt you have one of these 'coigns of vantage.' You see the busy town below, and hear its hum. On the one side are the suburbs where artisan and clerk and small tradesman have their long rows of cottages and houses, costing from £200 to £2,000 each, while on the other side are the high lands of Malvern and Toorak, where the successful squatter, speculator, and storekeeper have erected mansions, standing in at present prices from £5,000 to £50,000. Government House, the residence of His Excellency, the representative of the Crown, is a conspicuous object to the south; to the north is the handsome Exhibition Building, in which the gathering of 1880 was held. Numerous places of amusement speak of a pleasure-loving people. The two or three spires upon every hill proclaim a Christian community not averse to spending money and making sacrifices for its religion. There is no veneer. The cottage is usually of brick; the public buildings, from the twin cathedrals of the Roman and Anglican Churches downwards, are of stone, which is costly here. The mushroom Melbourne of 1857 has been exchanged for Mr. G. A. Sala's 'Marvellous Melbourne' of the present year of grace, 1886.

Melbourne streets are wide—a chain and a half or ninety-nine feet in all—and they are busy. The shops seem 'squat' to most visitors from the Old World, for two stories high was the rule until within the last few years; but as the price of land goes up, so does the height of the buildings. Nothing would be built in the city now under four or five stories, and there are tradesmen's places and stores and 'coffee palaces' that run up to six and seven stories, and are more than a hundred feet above the level of the roadway. Thus the complaint of squatness will speedily disappear. Not only are the streets wide, but they are also regular. Some run north and south; others east and west. Thus the city is something of a gridiron, or rather, giants could play games of chess upon its plan. Usually towns have been built on the tracks of the cows

A MELBOURNE SUBURBAN HOUSE.

of the first inhabitants, but Melbourne is a surveyor's city. All the streets are straight, and none would be narrow but that lanes intended by the original designers as back entrances for the residents of the main roads have been eagerly seized upon, and are utilised as business frontages. The importers of 'soft goods'—that is, of articles of apparel—have taken possession of one of these streets, Flinders Lane, and as 'the lane' it is known everywhere throughout Australia, without the need of any distinctive affix. Further north, dilapidated buildings in another 'lane,' with their shutters up and a profuse

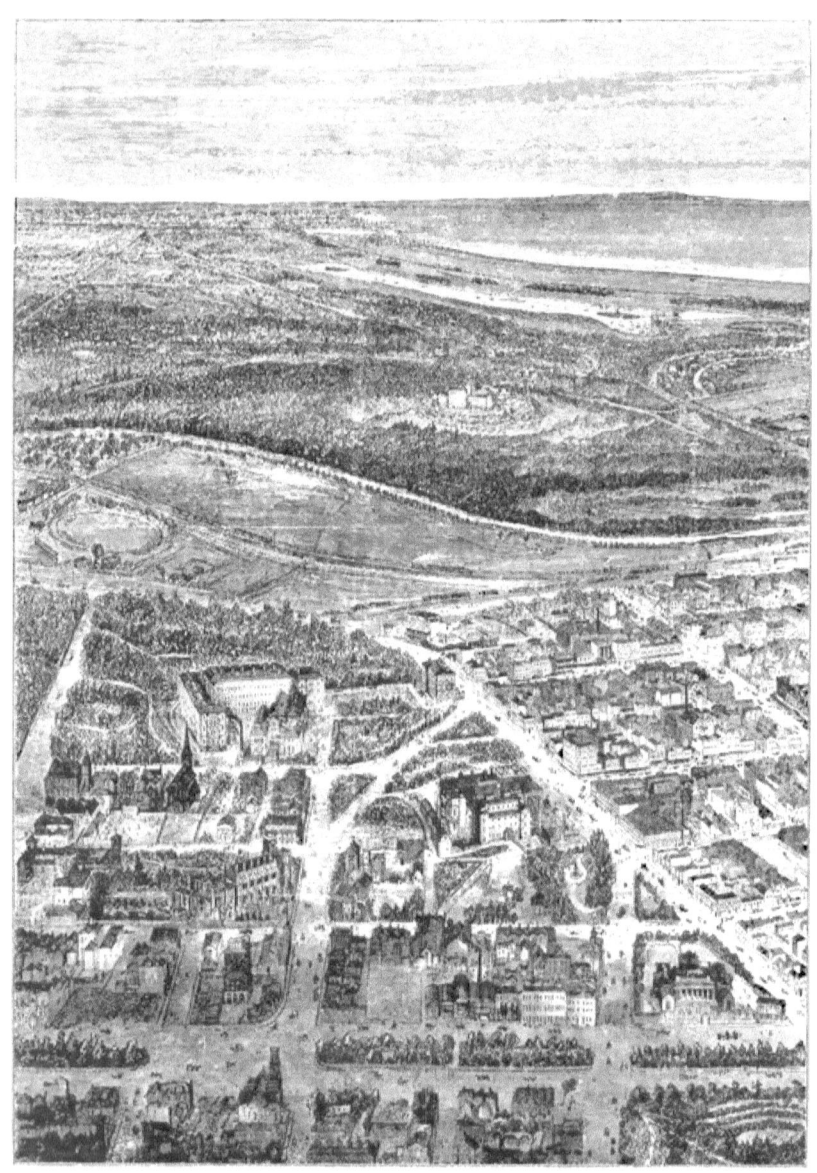

BIRD'S-EYE VIEW OF MELBOURNE, SHOWING PUBLIC OFFICES AND GARDENS; ST. KILDA IN THE DISTANCE.

BIRD'S-EYE VIEW OF MELBOURNE, LOOKING SOUTHWARDS TO THE SEA.

display of blue banners with golden hieroglyphics, proclaim that Little Bourke Street has been converted into a Chinese quarter. The main streets run their mile and more east and west. They are five in number, with four lanes, while nine broad streets run north and south. Of the five, Flinders Street is adjacent to the wharves and great warehouses, and is commercial in character.

Collins Street runs from the public offices in the east to the country railway-station in the west. The one end is given up to the fashionable doctors and the favoured dentists, handsome churches and prosperous chemists filling in the interstices. From the Town Hall corner, Collins Street is gay with carriages and with pedestrians who come to see or to shop. Farther on we enter the region of the banks, the exchange, the offices of barristers and solicitors, and the rooms of the auctioneers. Here men of business are hurrying about. The flutter about the tall building on the left tells of some mining excitement. Farther on, a bearded, sun-burned, but well-dressed group will attract attention. 'Scott's' is the squatters' hotel, and it has been selected as the place for submitting to auction those 'well-known and extensive pastoral properties entitled the "Billabong Blocks," within easy distance of market (say eight hundred miles), together with all improvements and stock.' The conversation is whether the station will bring £300,000 or not—for it is a large property; whether a better sale could have been effected in Sydney, and so on; and next day you read in your *Argus* that 'the biddings reached £290,000, when the lot was passed in, and was subsequently sold at a satisfactory price, withheld.' Last of all, in Collins Street come Assurance Companies' offices, the buildings of merchants, and great wool stores.

In Bourke Street, commencing again at the west, where the new Houses of Parliament stand, we have first shops, hotels, and theatres, then hotels and mews, and finally a region of hotels (now less frequent), and of offices and stores. Lonsdale Street is in a transitive condition. La Trobe Street is not recognised. Standing on the midway flat you see two hills: the western hill is commercial, the eastern hill is social. After six o'clock Flinders Street and Collins Street are deserted. In place of busy scenes of life there is gloom and solitude, while Eastern Bourke Street, where the theatres and concert halls are, is lit up and is thronged. Leisured people who can promenade in the day-time use Collins Street as their lounge; the toiling multitude, who must promenade in the evening or not at all, patronise Bourke Street. On Saturday nights the Bourke Street block is great; the footways will not accommodate the crowds.

Another Melbourne feature is the rush from the city from four to six o'clock P.M., and the inrush from eight to ten o'clock in the morning. It is enormous, but it is easily met. There is an extensive suburban railway system, the property of the Government—as all railways in Victoria are. Omnibuses and waggonettes are numerous, the latter taking the place of the London cab; and now there are gliding through the streets the successful and popular cable trams, a company having obtained a concession to put down fifty miles of these costly roadways. Let a heavy shower of rain fall at or about six P.M., however, and the rush is too great for the accommodation, and those 'too late' have to wait for return vehicles, and to bewail their misfortune.

BIRD'S-EYE VIEW OF CENTRAL MELBOURNE.

In public buildings Melbourne would be really great, if all that have been begun were finished. But few are. The citizens are not running up miserable flimsy structures, but are building for posterity. Final contracts have been taken for the Houses of Parliament, which are to be finished with a newly-discovered stone of a beautiful whiteness, but expensive to work. From first to last half a million of money will be spent on these halls of legislation. They will crown the eastern hill. The Law Courts, which cost nearly £300,000, are finished, and constitute a handsome pile on the western hill. St. Patrick's Cathedral, on the eastern hill, will be a marvel, and it is slowly

BOURKE STREET, MELBOURNE, LOOKING EAST.

creeping on. The Anglican Cathedral, founded by Bishop Moorhouse, is in the heart of the city, and is making more rapid progress. The Public Library is a noble institution, containing 150,000 volumes, and is open without restraint to all comers. So is a National Picture Gallery which is attached, and which contains specimens of the work of many of the best modern masters. There is a National Museum, in which the Australian fauna is admirably represented,

and the Melbourne University is near at hand. This institution, beautifully
situated and handsomely endowed, grants degrees which are recognised
throughout the Empire, and its doors are open to male and to female students
alike. Ladies have taken B.A. and M.A. degrees already, and the number
of the softer sex entering is on the increase. Not a ladies' school of repute
but has its matriculation class. The Town Hall, where 2,000 people can sit
to listen to the organ—one of the world's great organs—is not to be passed
over. The Botanic Gardens are another show spot. They are well within
the civic bounds, and by visiting them you obtain a series of lovely views,
and become acquainted with the flora of the Australian continent, for everything that can be coaxed to grow here has been provided by the director.

UNIVERSITY, MELBOURNE.

Mr. Guilfoyle, with a suitable home. There is a gully for the graceful
Gippsland ferns, a spot for the gorgeous Illawarra flame-tree, a guarded
receptacle for the great northern nettle-bush, which is here twelve or fifteen
feet in height, and which no one would presume to handle. Cycads, palms,
and palm lilies represent Queensland in one division ; a mass of foliage of a
bright metallic green speaks of New Zealand in another. Of no place is the
Melbournite more proud than of the Gardens, which Mr. Guilfoyle has only
had in hand about twelve years, but which he has transformed from a waste
into a Paradise.

Melbourne has a grand system of water supply. The river Plenty, a
tributary of the Yarra, is dammed twenty miles away, and the huge reservoir
when full contains nearly a two years' supply. The reticulation allows of a

supply of eighty gallons per head to each consumer; but in hot days the demand for baths and for the Garden are so great that this quantity is not found to be half enough, and improvements are to be effected. The Yan Yean system has cost £2,000,000, and now the Watts River is to be brought in, and as the engineers speak of £750,000 being necessary, the presumption is that £1,000,000 will be required. It is a grand spectacle to see a full head of Yan Yean turned on to a fire, say at night, when there is no strain to abate the maximum pressure. The flames are not so much put out as they are smashed out of existence. On a wooden building the jet will act like a battering-ram, sending everything flying. No engine is

THE FITZROY GARDENS, MELBOURNE.

required in these cases; the hose is wound on a light big-wheeled reel, and the instant an alarm is given a brigade can start off at racing speed and come into action on the moment of arrival.

As to industries, a list would be wearisome. A hundred tall chimneys make known to the observer the fact that Melbourne is becoming a great manufacturing centre.

The reserves between the city and its suburbs must ever be the greatest charm of Melbourne. To leave Melbourne on the south, you must pass through the mile-long Albert Park, with its ornamental water and its handsome carriage drives, or you must saunter through Fawkner Park or the Domain. Yarra Park and the Botanic Gardens are to the south-east, and they link with the beautiful Fitzroy Gardens. Carlton Gardens crown the city to the north, and communicate by smaller reserves, such as Lincoln Square, to the 1,000 acre Royal Park, in which, among other attractions, are the well-stocked gardens of the Zoological Society, open to the public on certain days, in consideration of a Government subsidy, free of cost.

The Yarra Park, lying between Melbourne and Richmond, contains the principal cricket grounds of the city. Here the Melbourne Cricket Club has its headquarters, and much its sward and its grand stand and its pavilion are praised by our cricketing friends from the Old World. In the season the big matches, All England *v.* Australia, or New South Wales *v.* Victoria, will draw their tens of thousands of spectators, and on other occasions the area is utilised for moonlight concerts, for flower-shows, and for pyrotechnics.

A jealous eye is kept upon these reserves. Once or twice a minister, eager to increase the land revenue, has made a dash at a city park, and has essayed to sell a slice, but so great has been the uproar that no Government is likely to indulge in the effort again. Indeed, in almost all cases, the alienation has now been rendered impossible except by means of an Act of Parliament, which could never be obtained. The belt of reserves—5,000 acres in all—is secure, and it must grow in beauty yearly, continually adding to the attractions of the town. As it is within a stone's throw of city life, you can wander into cool glens and sequestered shades, and hear the thrush sing, or study the beauties of a fern gully. To the pedestrian the walk to business in the morning or from it in the evening is thus rendered delightful; but if the ordinary Australian can possibly avoid it he never does walk. You meet curious traces in these reserves of that former time when the eucalypts sheltered not the inevitable perambulator and nursemaid at noon, nor the equally inevitable 'young people' at the 'billing and cooing' stage in the evening, but rather the kangaroo and the black fellow. In the Yarra Park an inscription on a green tree calls attention to the fact that a bark canoe has been taken from the trunk. The canoe shape being evident in the stripped portion, and the marks of the stone hatchet being still visible on the stem. The blacks would find their way to the river impeded now by a treble-track railway that runs close to their old camp, carrying passengers to a station which three hundred trains enter and leave daily.

Melbourne has a river. One knows this mostly by crossing the bridges, as otherwise the Yarra plays but a small part in the social arrangements of the community. The lower portion of the stream is being greatly improved. It is to be straightened and deepened, so that the largest liners are to come up to the city, as already do 2000-ton intercolonial steamers. The works, which will cost millions, are now (1886) about half-way through. Near Melbourne the stream is muddy and nasty. Sluicers use the water for gold-washing purposes twenty miles away, and factories were allowed years back to be started upon its banks, and though new tanneries and new fellmongeries are forbidden, the old evil-smelling establishments remain. Few who look upon the sluggish ditch at Melbourne would imagine that five and forty miles away it is a brisk and sparkling river, parrots and satin birds and kingfishers floating about it, ferns bending over and hiding its waters, and the giant gum rising from its banks to double the height of any city spire. The improvements will make the Yarra below the city a grand stream, bearing the commerce of the world on its bosom, and one may look forward to the time

THE YARRA YARRA, NEAR MELBOURNE.

when the city portion itself will be purified, and the river made worthy of its romantic mountain home.

The city has its drawbacks. There is dust in the summer, which the water-carts seek in vain to control; and there is mud in winter, which no raving against the Corporation appears to affect; and the less said on the drainage question the better. Again, as to weather, there are people who protest against the suddenness of the change when the wind in January chops round from north to south, and after panting in the morning you begin to think of a fire at night. But the three hundred delightful days of the year, when existence is a pleasure, are to be remembered, and not the odd sixty-five when ills have to be endured. A favourable impression is usually made upon visitors by the city with its charm of suburbs, its wealth and reserves, its crowds of well-dressed people, always busy about either their pleasure or their business, always obliging, the poorest showing no signs of poverty, nor yet the lowest of the influence of drink. And if a visitor had ideas of his own he would withhold any adverse dictum until he was away, and would not seek to wound the feelings of his hospitable hosts. With them, at any rate, it is a cardinal principle of faith that their much-loved home is entitled to the proud appellation of the 'Queen City of the South.'

An 'unearned increment,' such as would satisfy the most glowing dreams of the most ardent speculator, has occurred in the capital. One instance may be given. One of the few original half-acre blocks now in possession undisturbed—not cut up—of the family of the original purchaser is situated in a good part of Collins Street. The colonist whose executors are now holding the property gave £20 for it in 1837. To-day the sixty-six feet frontage to Collins Street is worth £1,150 per foot; the Flinders Lane frontage is worth £350 per foot. A little ciphering brings out a sum total of £99,000 as the present value of the original £20 investment. And for decades the income derived from the block has been counted by many thousands per annum. The £20 has by this time earned at least £200,000 in all. In many country places a £5 lot will bring £500 when a decade has passed. But then the place may not become a centre, and your 'unearned increment' will be no more substantial than the evening cloud. There is a reverse to this shield, as to all others.

From Melbourne it is easy to journey to the two great gold-fields of Victoria—Ballarat and Sandhurst. The latter is due north, and is reached by a double-track railway, built in the early days at a cost of £40,000 per mile. Single-track railways, costing £4,000 per mile, are now the order of the day. Sandhurst is the Bendigo of old days. It has had many ups and downs; has been deserted, and has been ruined; but the result is the fine city of to-day, with its broad, tree-lined streets, its splendid buildings, and high degree of commercial activity. As a recent writer puts it: 'What vicissitudes has not the place undergone! From enormous wealth to the verge of bankruptcy, from the pinnacle of prosperity to the direst adversity; from financial soundness to commercial rottenness; and yet, with that wonderful elasticity and buoyancy which characterises our gold-fields, the falling ball has rebounded, the sunken cork has again come to the surface, and Sandhurst, after all her reverses, is perhaps now richer and on a safer basis than ever—a city whose wide, well-watered streets are perfect avenues of trees, bordered by handsome buildings and well-stocked shops, brilliantly lighted by gas; whose hotel accommodation is proverbially good, whose

BIRD'S-EYE VIEW OF SANDHURST.

civic affairs are admirably regulated, whose citizens are busy, hospitable, and prosperous.' There is no mistake about the character of the town. Miles and miles of country before you enter it have been excavated and up-turned by the alluvial digger. And there are few more desolate sights to be met with than a worked-out and deserted diggings, for often Nature refuses to lend her assistance, and does not hide the violated tract with trees or verdure. Ugly gravel heaps, staring mounds of 'pipe-clay,' deposits of sludge, a surface filled with holes, broken windlasses, the wrecks of whims, all combine to make a hideous picture as they stand revealed in the pitiless sunshine. Alluvial digging of the shallow type is a curse to the unhappy country operated upon. But alluvial mining has long had its little day, and ceased to be in and about Sandhurst, and the town lives now by deep quartz mining. You come upon the 'poppet-heads' and the batteries everywhere, even in the beautiful reserve which is the centre of the city. Sandhurst contains 30,000 inhabitants, 8,000 of whom are miners, while the value of the mining machinery and plant is three-quarters of a million sterling.

Old Bendigo had busy scenes, but never did it witness such excitement as when a share mania broke out in 1871. Then it was that the richness of the so-called 'saddle reefs' was demonstrated. The old-established companies were paying well, and the Extended Hustlers exhibited one cake of 2,564 ozs. as the result of a crushing of 260 tons. This was just the spark wanted to set the market aflame. From being unduly neglected, Sandhurst was unduly exalted; new companies were projected in every direction where a line of reefs could be imagined; existing 'claims' were subdivided, and in a few months £500,000 was invested in Sandhurst mines. Of course there was a reaction; but though the speculators lost money to sharpers, there really were auriferous reefs in Sandhurst to be honestly worked, and no town seems more likely to hold its own in Victoria than the great quartz city. Foundries and potteries are springing up in its midst, or rather have sprung up; vineyards and orchards are found to be successes in its neighbourhood, and the visitor is grateful for the tree planting in the broad streets, appreciates the water supply, is duly dazed if he enters a battery chamber, and is delighted when 1,500 feet below the surface he is allowed to break off some fragment of glittering quartz.

Ballarat lies 100 miles to the north-east of Melbourne, or at least it is that distance by rail, viâ Geelong, but a direct line will soon reduce it to a distance of seventy miles. An upland plateau, with a fringe of hills all around, some of these now denuded of their timber, and glittering white, cold, and bare in the sun, the earth pitted with holes and gullies, scarified as if by some gigantic rooster, 'mullock'-heaps, 'poppet-heads,' and engine-stacks everywhere. This is one's first impression of Ballarat. Gold-fields are very much like each other all over the world. ' Substitute pines for eucalypti,' says Mr. Julian Thomas, 'and I could imagine this to be California. But when one first drives from the station and sees the magnificent width of Sturt Street, with the avenue of trees planted along the centre, the public buildings, banks, and churches—you are possessed with astonishment that this is a mining town. Ballarat is indeed a great inland capital. The difference between this and Sandhurst is that at the latter the mines obtrude themselves everywhere. One cannot go half a block but one has mullock-heaps and poppet-heads in view. There is a mine in every back-yard. At Sandhurst it is gold—nothing but gold! Small nuggets are occasionally, so say the truthful inhabitants, picked up by sharp-visioned pedestrians in the public streets. There is gold or evidences of it all around, even in the very bricks of the houses in which we live, for the old men tell that the first brick building ever erected in Sandhurst was pulled down and crushed, yielding three ounces to the ton! In Ballarat it is all different. Walk up Sturt Street, or along Lydiard Street, and one sees nothing but substantial buildings and avenues of trees. The mines are in the suburbs, and do not deface the town, as at Sandhurst. After an experience of the plains the city is a perfect Arcadia. Embowered in trees, the homes of the people are surrounded with gardens. There is verdure and vegetation in every street. One mentally associates an amount of roughness and coarseness with a mining town. Here it is quite other than so. There is everything to bring light and culture and sweetness home to the people. Sandhurst is superior in one respect—that its public gardens are right in the centre of the town, running by the side of old Bendigo Creek; but there is nothing in the colonies to surpass Wendouree Lake, the walks around it, and the adjacent reserves and Botanical Gardens. An easy walk from the town, and you embark on one of the fleet of elegant little steamers—perfect yachts—furnished with luxurious cushions and rugs as protection from the spray. Here everything is calm and peaceful. There is no dust, no noise, no smells. Sailing boats and rowing boats are plentiful; in little punts fishermen are bobbing for perch. This is a lung which gives health and happiness to the inhabitants of Ballarat. And when, after crossing the lake, you land under the shade of English oak trees, and the air is perfumed with the scent of new-mown hay, you feel that in no other mining community in the world have the people such privileges as here. The Botanical Gardens are always beautiful, and are a model to other establishments of the same kind in much larger communities.'

It was here, early in August 1851, that alluvial gold was discovered at a bend in the Yarrowee Creek, renamed Golden Point, where the toil of some of the earlier diggings yielded from twenty to fifty pounds weight of gold per day. In some spots, indeed, the gold lay almost on the surface, amidst the roots of the bush grass, to be turned up by the wheels of the passing bullock-drays, or picked out by hand after heavy showers. At first it was thought that the auriferous deposit did not extend beyond the commencement of the pipe-clay stratum, and most of the diggers moved further afield as soon as they had turned over the bare skin, so to speak, of the ground; but one digger, more persistent than the rest, dug beyond the clay, and was richly rewarded by finding that here lay the true home of the precious metal, here were the 'pockets' so dear to the heart of the true digger. The deserted 'claims' were quickly reoccupied, fresh thousands of diggers poured to the locality, and in a couple of months Ballarat was more vigorous than ever.

Then for a time it was thought that the golden riches lay solely in the alluvial stratum; but more modern research led to the discovery of a number of quartz reefs, from which large quantities of gold have been taken. Amongst the leading mines at present being worked are the celebrated 'Block Hill,' the 'Band and Albion,' 'Redan,' 'Washington,' 'Koh-I-Noor,' 'Band of Hope,' 'Victoria United,' 'Llanberis,' 'Smith's Freehold,' 'Williams' Freehold,' together with scores of others, employing upwards of three hundred steam engines, with an aggregate of about ten thousand horse-power, besides numerous machines worked by horses. The total value of the plant and machinery in use is nearly a million sterling, and the number of miners engaged in active operations is returned as nine thousand, of whom nearly one-seventh are Chinese. The total number of quartz reefs proved to be auriferous is between 350 and 400, while the extent of auriferous ground worked upon in the district is 187 square miles.

But, in addition to its mines, Ballarat is renowned for its pastoral and agricultural advantages, the Ballarat farmers being always large prize-takers at the various annual shows. The town is delightfully situated at an elevation of 1,413 feet above the sea-level, and is correspondingly healthy for all rejoicing in fairly robust constitutions. In winter the weather is sometimes of an ultra-bracing quality with sharp frosts, and even an occasional fall of snow, but on the whole the climate is very good.

'The Corner' is a local institution. It was at the Corner in olden days that a sort of open-air Stock Exchange was established, and here do speculators of all degrees still delight to come. Many are the stories of the fortunes that have here changed hands at a word—of the Midas-like touch of some, the Claudian fatality of withering blight possessed by others. Here, in the maddest times of the gold fever, was a scene of gambling pure and simple, as reckless as ever broke a Homburg bank. Here was the *auri sacra fames* in its most maddening and tantalising intensity. And here, even in these more prosaic times, are sudden flashes of the old spirit, that keep gesticulating crowds surging over the pavement, and the busy wires working hence to Melbourne, Sandhurst, and other commerce-hives.

Now and again we read of half-a-ton or so of gold being sent by one or other of the Ballarat banks to its Melbourne head office, and then we may be sure there is a bubbling over of excitement at the Corner. But it soon calms down to the ordinary seething of the cauldron, to which the shares of the various mining companies bob up and down with a regularity that can be almost reduced to a certainty.

Anthony Trollope said of Ballarat: 'It struck me with more surprise than any other city in Australia. It is not only its youth, for Melbourne is also very young; nor is it the population of Ballarat which amazes, for it does not exceed a quarter of that of Melbourne; but that a town so well built, so well ordered, endowed with present advantages so great in the way of schools, hospitals, libraries, hotels, public gardens, and the like, should have sprung up so quickly with no internal advantages of its own other than that of gold. The town is very pleasant to the sight.' And with these pleasant words we may leave the great mining capital.

If cities, like men, could enforce their rights by suits of equity, Geelong would be the capital of the colony of Victoria, and many heartburnings, past and present, would have been avoided. But as matters stand, Geelong has to be content with third place in the list of Victorian extra-metropolitan cities, and with a population of about 21,000. The claims of the town to greater consideration lie in its situation on the shores of Corio Bay, thus nearer to the sea than Melbourne, its central position as regards the first cultivated and most fertile district of the colony, and its early settlement. John Bateman, the pioneer, with his party of three white men and four Sydney blacks, landed at Indented Head on May 29, 1835, and would have 'squatted' thereabouts permanently had it not been for the proceedings of the aboriginals. As it was, Geelong was really founded as far back as 1837, when its site was planned by the then Surveyor-General, Robert Hoddle, and in 1849, or before the golden days, it was incorporated into a town. But fine harbour, excellent geographical position, and rich country at its back, were not enough to enable Geelong to compete in the race with Melbourne, Ballarat, and Sandhurst. It has grown truly, and the growth has been of the steady nature which gives flavour and solidity; but lacking the fertilising medium of gold, there is no luxuriance, no profusion. In the glorious future—the good time coming—this may prove to have been an advantage. At present it is regarded as a drawback. The town is in almost hourly communication with Melbourne, both by rail and steamer, and presents many other features showing it to be instinct with vitality of the best sort, and ready at any time to forge its way to the front.

Geelong exports goods, principally wool and produce, to the value of three-quarters of a million sterling per annum, and sends cargoes direct to London and Liverpool. To accommodate shipping three substantial jetties have been built at an expenditure of nearly one hundred thousand pounds, and the bar at the entrance of the harbour is kept clear to the depth of twenty-two feet. Another feature which strikes the eye of the visitor as he glances admiringly round the beautiful bay, on the shores of which the town sits enthroned, is the number of bathing establishments. There are no

ON LAKE WELLINGTON.

less than four of these, all of large size and comfortable appointments.

Geelong tweed has achieved a high reputation in many markets, and the shawls and blankets made in the town are also widely known.

After inspecting the gold-fields there can be no greater change for the visitor than to proceed to that Western District, far famed in Australia for the richness of its soil, the fineness of its pasture, and the soft beauty of its scenery. It is easily reached, for the railway now runs into its heart at Colac and Camperdown. This is the lake country of Victoria. An easy climb takes you to the top of the mount at Colac, and once there you can appreciate the description which Mr. Julian Thomas, the most popular descriptive writer of the Australian press, gives of the scene :—

'This lake country of Victoria,' says Mr. Thomas, 'possesses distinct features, distinct beauties, as yet unsung and unheard of except by the few. As I sit on a fragment of igneous rock and look around me, I indeed feel that "the singer is less than his themes." I feel that I cannot do justice to this magnificent view, I cannot describe all the pleasure it gives me. My readers must come and judge for themselves. We are on the edge of the extinct crater of an enormous volcano. Below us a number of lakes. Fresh and salt, some fifteen can be counted from this spot. They vary in size from the little mountain tarn filling up one of the mouths of the crater to the great dead sea, Corangamite, more than 90 miles round, and covering 49,000 acres. This lake is salter than the sea—no fish will live in its waters. From the Stony Rises on the south to Foxhow on the north its shores are outlined with jutting promontories—quaint and picturesque rocky curves, which give it additional beauty. Corangamite Lake is studded with islands, which increase its attractions by the variety of their form. On these, I am told, the pelicans, so numerous here, build their nests. Light and shadow are depicted in the reflections of passing clouds. The shores are white with accumulations of salt. Away in the north-west the dim, blue line of the Grampians. All around, hills and mountains—the Otway Ranges, Noorat, Leura, Porndon—are clearly defined. The park-like plains stretching away to the horizon are dotted with trees, under which thousands of cattle and sheep are sheltering from the rays of the noonday sun. Here and there pleasant homesteads, green cultivation patches, and fields of golden grain. But the especial glory of the scene is in the variety and number of the smaller lakes filling the craters below us. The yellow tints of the bracken covering the slopes are varied with green glints from the foliage of choice ferns on the steep banks, other colours being supplied by the mosses on the rocks. We have here light and shade, form, outline, colour—everything which makes up beauty in a landscape. And beyond that there is the wonderful interest in thinking of the past. Of the age when the numerous volcanoes in the west blazed forth their liquid fire over the land. Of the succeeding ages, when the craters, cooled and filled by springs, for century after century, shone in all their glory of lake and tarn under the actinic rays of the morning sun, which darkened the skin of the few black fellows camped on their banks. Now Coe Coe Coine, last King of the Warrions, has gone. We possess the land, with none to dispute our right to this earthly paradise. But the track of the serpent is even here. The enemy of mankind has now taken the form of the rabbit, which swarms around the Red Rock by the thousand.

'A strange feature in the lakes here is that they are alternately fresh and salt. Of five within gunshot of where we stand, three are salt and two fresh, yet they are separated only by narrow isthmuses. They vary also considerably in their height above sea-level. Corangamite is higher than Colac—these crater-tarns higher than Corangamite. There is a very high percentage of salt in some of these lakes. The saline properties are caused by the drainage from the basalt rocks, "the water being kept down by vaporisation, while the quantity of salt continually increases." In the summer the lakes fall by evaporation considerably below winter level, leaving on the banks large quantities of native salt in crystals, the gathering of which forms a remunerative occupation to many in the district. Cattle love this native salt, but Corangamite and its fellows are avoided by mankind. None bathe in their waters; no boats sail upon them. The large lake itself has

A VICTORIAN LAKE.

not even been surveyed or sounded. I am surprised that this has not been used for navigation. In the United States there would be steamers towing flat-bottomed barges; live stock and fire and pit wood, as well as passengers, would be conveyed from north to south and east to west; for, although shallow in places, there is ample depth for boats built on the American model. There was a tradition amongst the blacks that Corangamite and Colac were once dry, and again that at one time the lakes were all connected in one running stream. But whether the water privileges are sufficiently utilised or not, the lake scenery remains unequalled by anything I have yet seen.

F

The ports of this district are Warnambool and Belfast and Portland, and near the two first-named places is land of an exceptional richness that has gone far to make the locality wealthy. Here the potatoes of the continent are grown. Warnambool and Belfast supply the Melbourne, the Sydney, the Brisbane, and the Adelaide markets. There is no successful competition, for nowhere do quantity and quality go so well together. A

THE UPPER GOULBOURN, VICTORIA.

maximum yield of twenty and thirty tons per acre has been obtained. The land has been sold at £80 per acre. One landowner lets 1200 acres at £5 10s. per acre per annum. These are the 'top' prices, but they establish the fact that the volcanic formation of the Western District gives patches with a marvellous producing power. A small estate in *Australia Felix*—for it was this region which Mitchell so named—is a large fortune.

Portland Bay is the only harbour of refuge for hundreds of miles along the coast of Australia. As we steam in, Cape Grant shuts out the new lighthouse on Cape Nelson, the long swell is dashing with violence against the sides of Lawrence Rocks, whose peaks are the home of the gannet and other sea fowl. To the right at the extreme north is the flourishing rural township of Narrawong. Above this the green slopes of Mount Clay merge into the thickly-timbered forest land not yet cleared. Ahead there is a lighthouse, a signal post, a few houses embowered in trees, high cliffs of white limestone or dark basalt, and then, as we round the promontory into the harbour, the quaint yet lovely town is all before us, extending along the bluffs above the shore, the only natural depression being where a stream flows into the sea from a lagoon in a valley at the back of the town. The beauty of this crescent-shaped bay, with its outlines of bold headlands, is striking. As to the town, the white cliffs, the stone-built churches and houses, give it an English look. It recalls many spots on the Sussex coast. It is not Australian in any of its outer characteristics. The spirit of the English pioneer, Edward Henty, seems stamped upon it.

   Victoria is traversed for its greater part from east to west by a mountain chain, which is lofty in the south-east corner, Gippsland, takes the form of mere high land at the back of Melbourne, rises again in the Pyrenees, and dies out in the Western District. Usually the chain is about seventy miles from the seaboard. From the Gippsland sea-coast it presents a grand sight, often of snow-topped summits. Going to the north from Melbourne, you pass over the crest, which is 1700 feet high, without being aware of the rise. But all the water on the one side flows to the sea, and on the other to the river Murray. Crossing the range from Melbourne to the north and the north-east, the country slopes to the level Murray plains. Here you enter upon the wheat-growing district. The level ground is fenced into fields which bear this one crop. Shepparton, the agricultural centre of the north-east, aspires to be the Australian Chicago, and may be mentioned as an instance of the rapid changes which are possible in Australia. In a pictorial work published seven years ago, Mr. E. C. Booth writes: 'The township of Shepparton lies on the east bank of the Goulbourn. It gains its chief importance from the pound of the district being within its borders, and it will be remembered for years to come on account of the long and weary journeys to it undertaken by bullock-drivers and carriers in search of their strayed cattle.' How far off are those days now! Shepparton is to-day a local capital, busy and self-important. Its streets are lined with shops and houses; there are five banks, several assurance agencies, a handsome town-hall, and a busy traffic.

   What is said of Shepparton in the north-east applies to Horsham in the north-west. Horsham, the newly-created capital of the Wimmera District, is entitled 'the Prairie City.' The Wimmera climate is hot and dry, and there were doubts as to whether the farmer would hold his own on these arid plains; but the settlement is now twelve years old, and is increasing mightily. This Wimmera District tapers off into the mallee scrub, the old desert of Victoria, which has lain neglected for years, while Victorians have opened up country 2000 miles away. Here the dingo found his last refuge, and to the infinite joy of the dingo, as it may be supposed, the rabbit appeared upon the scene. When the rabbit came, the few squatters who were trying to turn the mallee scrub to account gave up in despair, for first the rabbits devoured the scant grass on which the sheep fed, and then the dingoes feeding on the rabbits grew more numerous and strong. The mallee went begging in blocks of 100,000 acres, at an annual rental of £5 per block; and at last the district had to be specially taken in hand by the State, and long leases have been granted to tenants on favourable terms, on condition that they destroy the 'vermin,' for that is the title bestowed upon rabbits here. Several rivers strive to flow from the ranges through or by the mallee to the Murray, but none succeed. The Avon, the Richardson, and the Wimmera all collapse and disappear on their way. The Loddon has a watercourse for the whole distance, but at its best in summer it will be but a chain of waterholes. Yet crop after crop is taken off these plains; the farmers all appear to make money, and now that works for conserving water for irrigation are to be undertaken, the spirits of these sunburnt toilers are of the highest.

WATERFALL IN THE BLACK SPUR.

All this district is intersected by 'wheat lines' of railway, over which in December, January, and February the crop is rushed to the seaboard. Great are the blocks that occur, and indignant is the grumbling because the whole yield cannot be carried at once. Horsham is hot with anger, and Shepparton refuses to be satisfied, and the lot of the Chairman of the Railway

Commissioners is not at this period to be envied. The railways run also to
the mountains of the east. One line will take the traveller to Beechworth,

A VICTORIAN FOREST.

a charming town in the north-east; another line will convey him to Sale
and soon to Bairnsdale—right away in Gippsland. Beechworth should be
visited because of the beauty of its surroundings. And if the visitor is a

pedestrian, he can accomplish a grand and quite a fashionable walking tour through the Alps into Gippsland, striking the railway either at Bairnsdale or Sale. He is in the neighbourhood of romantic ravines, picturesque waterfalls, and grand fern scenery. Lyre-birds, bower birds and parrots will be his companions, and if he chooses to diverge a little from the route, he may break into virgin solitudes, and may measure giant gums unheard of before.

One feature is common alike to all Victorian towns and the bush—the State school. In the towns the State school is a political structure. In the bush let there be twenty or thirty children in a three-mile radius, and there will be a wooden erection for the young people to attend. In some cases, where the children cannot be otherwise reached, the teacher will meet two or three families at intervals at certain houses. With a population of a million the State has 230,000 children on its school books. The instruction is 'free, compulsory, and secular,' and about this latter provision there is a great stir. It is not, however, advisable to stray into vexed issues here. Suffice it that there is no more general picture in Victoria, than that of the children trooping to and from their lessons, and that many a parent feels his existence brightened by the assurance that, come what may, 'schooling' is provided for.

Where there are no railways which the tourist can use, he may depend upon being able to proceed by 'Cobb.' 'Cobb' is the general name for the stage coach of the colonies, no matter who owns the vehicle, where it runs, what are its dimensions. Any one who has not travelled by Cobb has not properly 'done' Australia; and yet the fate of the black man and the marsupial will, one plainly sees, be the fate of Cobb. He will be improved out of existence, and thus another element of romance will fade away. Our illustrations tell their own tale of moving incidents by field and flood. Mr. Anthony Trollope wrote: 'A Victorian coach, with six or perhaps seven or eight horses, in the darkness of the night, making its way through a thickly timbered forest at the rate of nine miles an hour, with the horses frequently up to their bellies in mud, with the wheels running in and out of holes four or five feet deep, is a phenomenon which I should like to have shown to some of those very neat mail-coach drivers whom I used to know at home in the old days. I am sure that no description would make any one of them believe that such feats of driving were possible. I feel that nothing short of seeing it would have made me believe it. The passengers inside are shaken ruthlessly, and are horribly soiled by mud and dirt. Two sit upon the box outside, and undergo lesser evils. By the courtesy shown to strangers in the colonies I always got the box, and found myself fairly comfortable as soon as I overcame the idea that I must infallibly be dashed against the next gum-tree. I made many such journeys, and never suffered any serious misfortune.'

Why 'Cobb'? it may be asked. Freeman Cobb was an American driver of some New York express company, who came to Victoria in 1853 or 1854, and, seeing his opportunity, sent for some brother drivers and started coaches to Castlemaine and Sandhurst. For the hundred miles the fare was £8, and the money was well earned. Other coaches

STAGING SCENES.

followed in all directions. No Americans were needed to drive. It was found that the colonial-born youth had all the nerve and the spirit for dashing down the side of a gully, for steering along a siding, for fording a questionable creek, or for dodging fallen timber. Happily for the tourist, visits to some of the show places of Melbourne are still partly paid by coach. To see the romantic falls of the Stevenson and the silver eucalypts of the Black Spur, a partial coach journey is necessary. At Loutit Bay Waterfalls,

A SHARP CORNER.

the ocean and the big trees are all brought together, and to reach this favoured and favourite spot the coach must be utilised. It was well for the nerves of Mr. Anthony Trollope that he was not required to perform this particular journey, Lorne or Loutit Bay not having been opened up when he was on the land. The coaches cross a succession of ranges running up to 2000 feet in height, and they had to shave with remarkable closeness some of those gums whose nearness alarmed the English author. One rush down a steep siding was made between two giant eucalypts. There was just room to pass, but so little to spare that the axle on the off side had cut a track through the one tree by the process of frequent touching. If it had touched too hard the passengers would have picked themselves up after a drop of several hundred feet. Or they might have had a grand flight through the air into the midst of the fern jungle that hid a purling stream far, far below. The rush through the twin eucalypts was exhilarating; the steerer of Cobb, a native of the place, cool and confident, enjoyed it immensely.

NEW SOUTH WALES.

VIEWS IN SYDNEY: GOVERNMENT HOUSE, THE CATHEDRAL, AND SYDNEY HEADS.

GOVERNMENT BUILDINGS, MACQUARIE STREET, SYDNEY.

CHAPTER V.

NEW SOUTH WALES.

SURVEY OF THE COLONY—SYDNEY AND ITS HARBOUR—THE GREAT WEST—THE BLUE MOUNTAINS—THEIR GRAND SCENERY—AN AUSTRALIAN SHOW PLACE—THE FISH RIVER CAVES—DUBBO TO THE DARLING—THE GREAT PASTURES—THE NORTHERN TABLELAND—THE BIG SCRUB COUNTRY—TROPICAL VEGETATION.

NEW SOUTH WALES is the mother colony of Australia, and though, after the gold discovery, she was for a time thrown into the shade by the prowess of her former dependency, Victoria, she is making rapid strides to recover; in fact, she may be said to have regained her old premier position. Her eastern boundary is the Pacific Ocean, which washes a coastline of 800 miles, bold in its outline and studded with numerous harbours. Imaginary lines divide her from Victoria to the south, Queensland to the north, and South Australia to the west. The greatest length of New South Wales is 900 miles; its greatest breadth about 850 miles; mean breadth, 600 miles. The superficial area is 309,100 square miles. That is to say, the colony is as extensive as the German Empire and Italy combined, or as France and the United Kingdom. The million of population which the colony contains is thinly scattered about this vast territory, the country districts obtaining the less, because more than a third of the people are congregated at Sydney, the capital, and at Newcastle, the coal port adjacent to the metropolis. High mountain ranges are found in New South Wales, lofty tableland, and vast low-lying plains, with the result that great variety of climate is obtained. For instance, on a certain day in November, 1885, the newspapers state that between the Warrego and the Paroo, north of the Darling, one thousand out of five thousand sheep had dropped dead upon a rough day's journey, wasted by the hunger and drought, and killed by heat; that two out of a party of three travellers perished of thirst in the Lechlan back blocks, and the third alone, naked and half mad, reached a station to tell the tale; that on the lower reaches of Clarence and Richmond rivers travellers saw cattle in the last stages of starvation, dying in the mud of the river banks, while down upon the Shorehaven a roaring spate was heaving haystacks to the sea; that while enterprising tourists were chilled with ice and sleet upon Ben Lomond, and snow was flattening crops of wheat in the gullies above Tumat, Sydney, despite the coolness of the daily inflow of ocean water, was suffering under a heavy sweltering heat. And while variations like these are the exception and not the rule, yet all these varied experiences may be endured in the colony on one and the same day.

New South Wales was discovered and named by Captain Cook, who landed in Botany Bay, a few miles north of Port Jackson, on the 28th of April, 1770. A penal settlement was formed the following year, and four days after the arrival of the little fleet, a French expedition, under the ill-fated M. de la Pérouse, cast anchor in the bay. The officer in command, Captain Arthur Phillip, soon recognised that Botany Bay was in many respects unsuitable for a principal settlement; and having examined Port Jackson, and found it to be 'one of the finest harbours in the world,' he did not hesitate to substitute it as the position from which to commence Australian colonisation. On the 26th of January, 1788, the fleet and all the people were transferred to Port Jackson; a landing was made at the head of Sydney Cove (the Circular Quay), and the colony of New South Wales was formally declared to be founded. The first settlers in all numbered 1030, of whom 504 were male exiles and 192 female exiles. On the 7th of February Arthur Phillip, Captain-General and Governor-in-Chief of the new territory, established a regular form of government; and, in his address to the assembled colonists, expressed his conviction that the State, of which he had laid the foundation, would, ere many generations passed away, become the 'centre of the southern hemisphere the brightest gem of the Southern Ocean.' The peculiar audience which he addressed did not share his enthusiasm, but the prediction has been abundantly realised. The convict

STATUE OF CAPTAIN COOK AT SYDNEY.

stage is now forgotten as a dream. To-day New South Wales contains almost a third of the population of all the colonies, has an annual import and export trade of nearly £50,000,000, and raises annually £9,000,000 of revenue. The colony has already constructed 1727 miles of railway, and is constructing 416 miles, and Parliament has authorised the construction of 1282 miles, and there are 19,000 miles of telegraph wires open. The value of its annual export of wool is, in normal seasons, worth £10,000,000; its sheep number 35,000,000; its horses, 350,000; its horned cattle, 1,500,000; and its swine, 220,000. The land under crop is 1,000,000 acres; the annual out-put of coal is 3,000,000 tons, of which nearly two-thirds are exported. The mines of gold, silver, tin, copper, and manganese, are also very rich, and their export is great. The city of Sydney and its suburbs have a population of 270,000.

The following general description of Sydney and the colony is contributed by Mr. F. H. Myers:—

'Naturally any notice of the colony of New South Wales begins with Sydney and its harbour—

> "Like some dark beauteous bird whose plumes
> Are sparkling with unnumbered eyes,"

wrote Moore, as he looked up aloft at the sky by night, and found companionship in the soul of beauty there. Often has the image occurred to me when entering, on a summer's night, the harbour gates of Beautiful Sydney, or looking down upon the stillness of the sleeping coves from any of the surrounding hills. Lights are spread upon the blackness of the hills —straight lines, crescents, squares, and marvellous configurations—lights rise up from the harbour depths, straight shafts and twisted columns, pillars and spires and trees of light, wherever from ship's mast, or yard, or port, rays of white or blue or red strike the waters, and straightway seem to grow as plants of fire. Along the shores may be seen the blue gleams of electric fire, the duller green and red of the oil lamps on the ships, still and bright in the quiet water; alternating, mingling, shifting, blending, as the surface is only slightly stirred. Every calm night brings such illumination.

'A traveller entering Sydney Harbour upon any still night sees this panorama opening to him; and if he have the good fortune to be detained in quarantine till morning, he may see a far more beautiful picture by rising with the rising sun. The city and the harbour lie spread out before him, the spires and towers standing out in the distance, clear and shining in the morning sunlight. The long land arms run out on either hand, while the blue sea, unruffled and smooth, forms a fine contrast to rock and foliage and sky.

'To see Sydney well in the clear broad daylight, it is needful to travel by the cable tram to the heights of North Shore, and walk thence by the military road to the head of Morsman's Bay. A splendid view point is thus obtained, above and opposite to the length and breadth of the city. You see the light-tower upon the Moth Head, and following the coast-line south you look along all the heights of Woolahra, Waverly, and Paddington to Randwick. Between that ocean coast and the inner line of the harbour are the homes of a quarter of a million of people. You may see thence the

THE POST OFFICE, GEORGE STREET, SYDNEY.

spires of St. Philip's, and St. James', and St. David's, and St. Patrick's, the towers of St. Andrew's Cathedral, and, through the heavy foliaged trees of the domain, the high walls of the yet unfinished St. Mary's. In the distance, and partly obscured by the smoke of the University buildings, the various colleges are grouped, almost joined by the distance. Near them are the Prince Alfred Hospital, and the deaf, dumb, and blind institutions.

G

Sydney Harbour.

'In the dense centre of city buildings rises the new tower of the General Post Office. It overlooks everything, and waves its flag of practical utility in the sight of the whole city. Very near to it appears the Town Hall, small by comparison, though more elaborate, and between them and the

MACQUARIE STREET, SYDNEY.

water the heavy masses of commercial buildings fringed by the unbroken line of masts. The city yet to be on the North Shore looks very small, and you are not surprised that no suspension bridge overhangs the water. You must look into the future for that.

G 2

'Complete your picture of the present by a glance up the long estuaries of the Paramatta and Lan Cove rivers, and a look across the rolling woodlands westward to the giant barrier of the Blue Mountains. Look also across the harbour, where right below you the round tower of Fort Dennison stands in mid-channel, and a little lower down the perfect half moon of Rose Bay, blue as the sky above. Look down to the Heads, where a dozen craft are entering upon the long huge rollers which break upon bluff Dobroyd opposite, or die down to ripples upon the innumerable beaches of Middle Harbour. Watch the many lights and colours of the water, the ultramarine of the mid-channel, the indigo in the shadow of the hills, the emerald of a strip close beneath the cliff, where no wind moves, nor any pulse of tide or ocean stir is felt; the glories of opal and amber, where fierce sun rays burn about rocky shores.

'Take in all the greatness and beauty of the present, and then try to realise the picture in the square miles of buildings already raised. You can see how they are growing, how far away to south and west, and through the forest and beside the waters of the north coast, houses and establishments of various kinds are rising like *avant couriers* of the compact masses whose advance is by no means slow. Look from them to a point of the city where roofs and chimneys are most closely packed, where the smoke of the labour of human life seems ascending perpetually, and you may see a succession of white puffs, and hear a louder, sharper pulse of toil pierce the low murmur of distant and multitudinous sounds, and you know that you look upon the present centre of the railway system of the colony; you have fixed your eye upon the focussing point of two thousand miles of railways. These are the feeders of the city; these reaching out divide and grip and drain the colony. They gather its produce, the results of its labour, and bring them down to this city, which stands without rival or competitor along 800 miles of coast.

'Let us travel along each of these lines, radiating somewhat as the fingers of a spread hand from south to north.

'The South Coast Railway, the most recently opened and not yet completed line, runs down the south coast to Kiama. This line is a purveyor of many luxuries and necessaries of life, leading out first to broad suburban breathing grounds on the country between the southern bank of Port Jackson and Botany Bay, making a hundred square miles of good building country accessible, crossing the historic bay three miles up the tidal estuary of George River, crossing a somewhat barren plateau, and arriving at the National Park. It penetrates next vast forests and overruns tremendous gorges, winding about precipices, and getting down by a way of its own to the country at the foot of the Bulb Pass. All the seaward slopes and ravines of this pass are as a vast natural conservatory. They take all the morning sun, they are never touched by western or southern wind, they are plentifully watered

THE TOWN HALL, SYDNEY.

with regular rains, and they nurse and produce a beauty unfamiliar to the latitude. Take a few steps over the brow of the hill on the old road, and look down. You see tropical verdure and bloom, palms rising a hundred feet, and spreading feathery plumes upon lance-like stems; myrtle and coral trees, figs and lily-pillies, with a sheen upon their leaves like the light on a summer sea; bowers and arches and impenetrable jungles of great vines, trailing tendrils fifty feet long, and swinging masses of perfumed bloom a hundred feet from the ground. There is nothing of the old familiar Australian bush about it. You are 1,200 feet above the sea, which stretches away to the world's rim beneath and before you. Below, past all the wonderland of the bush, is the white tower of Woolongong, and beyond that the fringe of white beach and snowy breakers, the Fern Islands, set in sapphire. Far, far away goes the coast land.

'Between coast-line and mountains lies the fertile land, the strip of country that serves and feeds the great city. The train comes here to be laden with the rich produce—milk, butter, and cheese—which by tons upon tons is taken in and distributed in Sydney every day. Out of the bowels of the mountains the line brings also coal and iron and shale and other mineral products, and from the dense forest pour down the little coast rivers.

'Halting at Kiama first, it will render all the beauties of the Illawarra district proper accessible, as all its rich products available; but in a very few years it must pass on across Shoalhaven and Begar, and over the rugged country of the Victorian border beyond Eden and Boyd Town.

'Our next finger, The Great West, is a mighty one in every sense, 574 miles in length, and crossing in that length a fair section of the whole colony, and enclosing in the triangle of which it forms the northern side, with the Southern and South-Western line and Murrumbidgee river opposite, and the Darling for base, the wildest mountains, the richest agricultural acres, and the broadest pastures of the colony. By Paramatta, Castle Hill, and Toongabbie, the earliest agricultural settlements the colony knew, which, however, seem rather to have reached senility than perfect development, the North-Western line strikes out for the rampart of the famous Blue Mountains—now one of the show-places of Australia. Very soon the traveller perceives the great barrier stretched right across the plain. Behind the dark green trees of the middle distance it looms as the wall of some forbidden land. And nearer the deep blue river at its feet looks like a moat specially made for purposes of defence. Long indeed was the barrier effective, before the strong right arm of civilization put down the stone pillars and carried over the platform of the railway-bridge across which the train thunders now, the great engines puffing and snorting, their force conserved for the present, but ready to be expended by-and-by in the charge up the mountain.

'The upward view from that bridge should never be missed. It is a long glassy sheet of water, coming from the bold and densely timbered gate of the hilly shore miles away, and flowing down to the bridge, past the sleepy old town, between grassy banks or drooping willows, or groves of whispering oaks. There is no perceptible current, the water-lilies sleep on the surface, and if a boat be pulling upwards the ripples of the water break gently on either bank.

You may note so much in the rapid transit of the train, which ten minutes after its departure from Penrith station is fairly at

EMU PLAINS.

the feet of the mountains. There are little knolls there, lightly grassed and gracefully timbered, looking down upon

"Long fields of barley and of rye."

Very soon we pass these fields; we are rising fast. The plains sink and extend beneath us. The white stones of the little grave-garden at Emu Plains glisten beside the tall black cypress trees, the river shines like a band of steel, and the reflection of the willows and oaks are faintly seen.'

Penrith looks as a child's toy village; and Windsor and Richmond, far away, are but indistinct white dots. All quiet, tame, prosperous, and very

THE VALLEY OF THE GROSE.

simply beautiful below; all above and beyond wild and rugged, and, in the commercial sense, unprofitable. As marvellous a contrast as could be imagined, the beginning and the end apparently of new orders, the results of different forces, the work of the earth spent in opposite moods. One must needs marvel in contrasting such scenes, and more profound becomes the marvel and the wonderment, as with every mile a vaster, wilder, grander region is found. Cliff-faces leagues long, and a thousand feet perpendicular; huge basins, like veritable gulfs in space, where a firmament of blue gathers between the rocky mountain head and the forest growth below, isolated rocks that dwarf all monuments reared in any city of old; deep calling unto deep in innumerable waterfalls, and through all the summer months frequent thunder, as if the spirits who had wrought their marvels below were still toiling at some other labour in mid-air. The meanest mind becomes expanded in wonder, and the least philosophical instinct begins to speculate and inquire. There has, indeed, been much deep speculation, much zealous and competent inquiry as to the phenomena of these mountains, and the startling contrast upon their southern front. Tennison-Woods studied and wrote of them, and more recently Dr. J. E. Taylor has, in a few graphic sentences, expressed his opinions of the geological changes which have taken place, particularly of the changes and causes which have produced the fertile plains and the hills, whose chief present product is ozone, with the river rolling between. Having touched lightly upon the facts generally known of the Hawkesbury sandstone formation, overlaid on a great breadth of the county of Cumberland by the Wianamatta shales, he says:—

'But the continuity of both the Hawkesbury sandstones and the overlying and usually accompanying Wianamatta shales is interfered with on a magnificent scale at Emu Plains. The entire country from this point to Sydney Heads has been slowly let down by one of those great earth movements known as a "downthrow fault." The downthrow was not the work of one single act of disturbance—it went on for ages. Meantime the Wianamatta shales, which overlaid the Hawkesbury sandstones of the Blue Mountains, were denuded off, or nearly so, for there is only a small patch now remaining, right on the top, after we have ascended by the first zigzag, to show that they were once continuous with those of the plains more than 2,000 feet below.'

There is infinite variety in the mountains. Even though wearied of the grandeur and wildness of the gorges, the vastness of the basins, whose great forest carpets appear but as robes of green evenly spread, or the grotesquely piled rocks, and the bold and beautiful flora of the tablelands and mountain heads, the traveller need not hasten back to town, imagining he has seen all. Let him find his way down from Blackheath to the entrance of a valley known as the Mermaid's Cave—a great grey rock that juts out and almost blocks the valley, dividing a somewhat arid gorge above from a lovely dell below. He passes through a rock-cleft, and there before him is a scene beautiful as new. There indeed,—

'A vale of beauty, lovelier
Than all the valleys of the greater hills.'

Yes, this is the fairy land of the mountains. Tall, feathery-foliaged, golden-blossomed wattles rise side by side with the olive-green turpentines, and through them runs the mountain brook in cataract after cataract. Upon the edge of the wattle-grove the tree-ferns grow, and beyond them is a carpet of bracken—a broad slope at the hill-foot, rich dark green with tips of pink, and shadows and hollows of russet and brown, where new growths display yet their dainty shades, or dead leaves have taken the rich autumnal brown.

There is deep, grateful shade here in the heat of the day, for no sunbeam penetrates the roof of wattle and palm-like fern, and the water seems to bring down coolness from its higher springs.

A bolder valley, one of the great gorges of the world, is the Lithgow, the road to the western slopes and the long-locked interior. It was down this great ravine that the first explorers looked awe-stricken at the marvellous road that nature had prepared for them ; and who can gaze without awe and wonder and broadening conceptions of nature and nature's work as he looks down that entrance way to Australia's heart, and realizes the manner and the period of its making? The ages that have clothed the mountain sides with forests are but as seconds to years by comparison with

ZIGZAG RAILWAY IN THE BLUE MOUNTAINS.

those which have worn the world's crust away, and by comparison with these stupendous results of natural forces, what pigmy work appears the zigzag down which goes the inland train ! This Lithgow Vale is usually considered the western limit of the Blue Mountains, though in their further northward range, notably about Capertee on the Mudgee line, they rise again and display forms of rugged grandeur.

Beyond the mountains the artistic surveyor may travel fast. Branching off at Walerawang, he may find the mountain scenery he has just left repeated on the line to Mudgee, but there is another turn, and not by rail, which he must not miss. It is at Tarana, in the Fish River Caves, newly christened Jenola. The road runs off to the southward, a distance of forty miles, to the west of a wild country on the western slopes of the Blue Mountains, and then by a grim cavern in the hill-side is entry found to a natural temple, which travellers affirm has no equal in the wide, wide world. The old guardian and guide of the place, who alone can walk safely amid the labyrinth, tells us that we have hardly begun to explore the caves so far, for every year some new grotto is discovered. He plods his careful way along some dripping track through the tall stalagmites, standing as monuments of the dead in fairy-land, feels some fissure in the mountain side, works the point of his staff through, and discovers—vacuity; makes carefully a small hole, introduces a thread of magnesium wire, sets it ablaze, and in the long glow learns that he has discovered another cathedral vaster than St. Peter's, with a dome that mocks St. Paul's. By-and-by he will open a way to it; will add it to his catalogue; will say to a party of visitors: 'I have found another

FISH RIVER CAVE.

cave, and will flash light upon the glory which, could it be transported to London or Paris, would be worth a million sterling.' How many more caves remain to be discovered it is impossible to say; they may run miles into the mountains. Future days may see mimic electric cars running through the caves, and brilliant globes of light flashing like suns upon the summits of tall lone columns ten miles from the entrance. Now there is no tramway nor riding way whatever within the caves, but difficult foot-paths and painful steps, and slightly hazardous creeping places, and ladders to ascend, and narrow parts to pass, and a good deal of labour to be performed to see even a little of the treasures which have so far been unlocked. There are, to the traveller who has leisure and who is content to live hard and sleep hard, so that he may delight his more refined faculties, four days' good sight-seeing in the caves—four days through which the world and all the things therein may be left behind, and glories as of a kingdom of old may be fully enjoyed — four days through which he may imagine himself entering into such a land as that held by Lytton's 'Coming Race,' domes of the world above you vast as the dome of heaven without. Far down below the strange black river, running—

'Through measureless caverns to the sea;'

mysterious echoes meeting you, great white ghostly figures appearing suddenly in the fitful illumination, alabaster lakes, pools, baths, spotless, stainless marble sanctuaries, and palace halls, which, lit by the sudden flash from the magnesium wire, seem bespangled more thickly and gorgeously than any royal crown with glittering jewels. You are filled rather with wonderment than admiration, and the whole world without seems utterly contemptible to you, whenever you return to the cave's mouth.

WATERFALL AT GOVETT.

There are green fields at the bases of great timbered hills all the way to Bathurst, where the oldest and most considerable of all inland cities of the colony sits beside the Macquarie river, on the crown of the down country which rolls, rich with grass or grain, for leagues around. On the long north-eastern flight we may hover a while over Bathurst, may note with pleasure the fair country homes amongst the gardens and bowers, the church spires of the city, and the many fair buildings. We shall not find another such town as Bathurst, though country fair enough is beneath us by Blayney and Orange, and southward thence through many villages and little mining towns to Forbes. And almost due north to the Wellington valley, and out to Dubbo, which is the gate of the great pastures, the country is of the same character.

On leaving Dubbo we reach the magnificent distances of Australia, the land of the mirage and the great drought, the land of marvellous flocks and herds. There on the vast bush plain or amongst the box forest are great hosts of cattle, one or two or three thousand head, already six or nine months on the road, hoping to make the port or the trucking station in three months more. Strange men are with them, white as to colour—as white in pluck and endurance, but as uncivilised as the one or two trackers who watch the horses. In this region during the bad seasons you cross bare and bone-strewn plains. At a wretched homestead you may find a man in the lowest deep of despair. Well-to-do a couple of years ago, hoping to be rich before the decade had closed, he is lord now of twenty thousand skeletons lying upon the soil, which looks as if indeed cursed, and so effectively that it will never bear grass or herb again. You may see river-beds of baked mud, and glistening veins of sand that once were running creeks. Here grow brigalow and mulga, gaunt and weird as the dragon-tree of the Soudan. Hundreds of miles stretches this dreary land, the Lachlan winding through it from east to west, the least significant stream in a dry or ordinary season that ever served as the watercourse for so broad a land.

Out in its centre lies a village, Cobar, grown about a mountain of copper, and along the Darling are other villages, Bourke, Bremoroma, Welcanna, Wentworth, lingering on when no rain falls, and blossoming with a dripping month as rapidly almost as the herbage of the black flats. I never saw anything beautiful in them except the self-devotion of some few good women who shine as stars amongst the general blackness. But when the rain has fallen, particularly in the pleasant winter after a genial autumn, it cannot be said that the land lacks beauty. I remember winter days a hundred miles north and south from the Darling river at Bourke, when the face of nature seemed to shine in open placid beauty and to break into the tenderest imaginable smile with each dying day; mornings in June, when, awakened by the glowing log to see the flush of dawn through an oak hut or over a pine-ridge that seemed to rise mysteriously with the sun, and, as though actually molten down by the increasing heat, to vanish utterly in the full glow of day. There was no painful mockery in the mirage that hung at noon on the horizon, with its flat-crowned trees rooted apparently in the still blue water—for by any clump of broad-leaved colane or drooping myall there was water in abundance, water clear and cool in every hollow; and grass, herbage and flowers knee-deep over all the land, when the spotted leaf and trees were all abloom and the quandongs were heavily fruited, and the nardoo with its life-saving seed ripened and decayed unheeded. Often at eventide in that winter did the whole landscape seem pure and perfect as a single crystal, the sky just after sunset of the palest primrose or the colour of the neck of a wheat-stalk when the ear is just ripe ; the flood water through the lignum bushes glassy still ; not a leaf of any tree stirring nor a grass-blade or herb-bloom moving upon all the plain. From the multitudinous flowers of the sand-ridge comes a rare sweet fragrance mingling with the balsamic odour of the pines. There would be noise and tumult a little later, as the crested galahs came cackling homeward to rest, and then the long and solemn hush of night, with sound enough and yet no lack of peace. The whistle of the wild duck's wing and sharp blow of her descent on the water, the dull thunder of the wings of great birds—pelicans, native companions, swan, ibis, and crane—rising in hurried flight, scared by some movement of 'possum or night-feeding kangaroo. Always the tinkle of the horse-bell and the prattle of the flame-tongues within the little circle of heat and light. Beauty enough in the inner lands in such a year, a marvellous contrast to the ghostliness, the abomination of desolation, of the year when no rain falls and all life dies.

The northern table-land is intersected by the Great Northern Railway, and is bounded by the Pacific Ocean, the Macpherson range, the Dumaresque and Darling rivers, and the Great Western line. The third division of the colony contains upwards of 100,000 square miles of country, of mountain and plain and wild forest and fertile down, and infinite variety of scenery. Near to the coast, and south and west from the line leaving Newcastle for the north, such country as we have seen about Orange and Albany, but with the green in foliage and verdure which comes from a somewhat warmer and more genial climate. Farther inland there are more of the great pastures, and in the extreme north a prosperous agriculture and a beginning of tropical industry, which afford a pleasant contrast to all that we have seen before. We shall not linger long here to look upon any New England villages or prosperous towns. We shall not concern ourselves with the marvellous richness of the Breeza plains—where in the wet summers grass grows so tall that horses and bullocks are lost ; and stockmen tell of patches where they have had the long seed-stalks above their heads, and they on horseback—but visit the north-eastern corner of the colony, where the three sugar rivers come down from the mountains.

All their surroundings are tropical and rich, and never so rich perhaps as in the heart of the country lying about the heads of the Richmond, and northward towards the Tweed River. There we find the vegetation whose density and glory and magnificence must be seen to be realised. It is the country known as the Big Scrub, where everything is gigantic, compared with ordinary Australian vegetation. The river flows deep and navigable for small craft between low banks of rich deep soil, chocolate loam, decomposed trap rock, spouted in remote ages from the mountains whose high wild crests overlook the Queensland country, a hundred miles to the north. The dense scrub growth covered all a half-century ago, and the huge cedar-trees towering above the jungle overhung the river; but now along many a mile the scrub has been cleared away, and the cane-fields surround the settlers' houses. Wonderfully delicate and fair look the canes beside the dark scrub, bright green or pale yellow, as varied in tint as wheat-fields between the time of the bloom and the harvest. They give grand evidence of the power of the soil, and fully justify the wisdom of those bold speculators who built the great mills lower down.

Quickly changes the foliage as the ascent to the table-land is made; vines and flowers and orchids are left behind. Pine and cedar give place to gum, box, and ironbark, while in the gullies are ferns of a hardier growth, and trickling water that seems of near relationship to the mountain snows. Higher and higher, and colder and fresher becomes the air; and, turning now, the panoramic view below spreads broad and fair, the half-dozen branches of the Richmond seen flashing at times through the trees, the corn and cane patches but bright green dots in the dense forest, and braids of a lighter green beside the broader stream, a reflection of the ocean upon the farthest sky; and last, upon the heights the distant northern mountains are seen the giant warders of the Great Divide. Mount Lindsay is the grandest of all, lifting crags and ramparts more than 5,000 feet from the downs below, as rugged in appearance as any escarpment of the Blue Mountains, and of a vaster height and bulk. The rich pasture-lands about his feet are buried in haze, and occasional lagoons sparkle like flakes of silver or eyes of a well-contented earth-spirit looking up to the sky. Waiting there till evening, you may see Mount Lindsay afire with the floods of light which catch his summit when all the trees below are dark; and farther south, where the Clarence River springs, the tall gaunt peak of the Nightcap will only lose the light before the mightier mountain. Both stand out above all neighbours, though joining them is a mighty chain, with beauties innumerable, stretching right along the line which separates the tropic land of Queensland from the beautiful and prosperous colony of New South Wales.

SOUTH AUSTRALIA

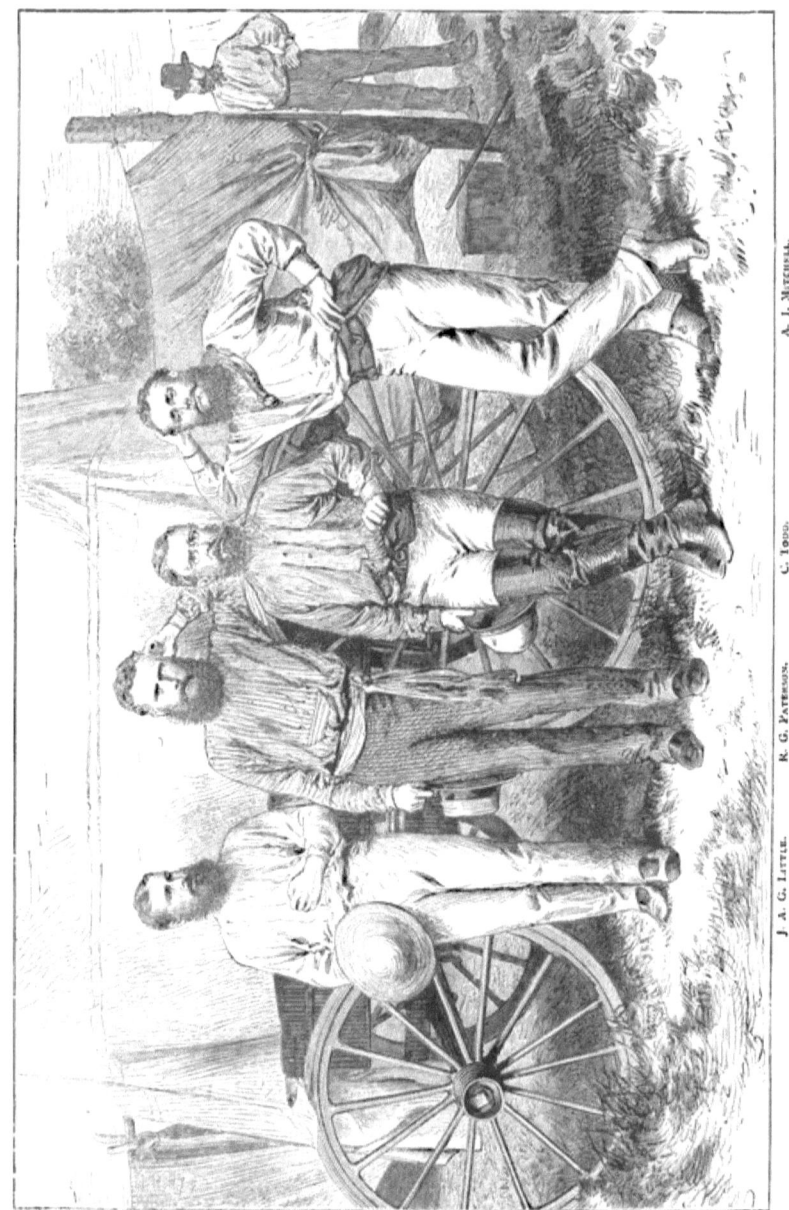

J. A. G. LITTLE.   R. G. PATERSON.   C. TODD.   A. J. MITCHELL.
OVERLAND TELEGRAPH PARTY.

GOVERNMENT HOUSE AND GENERAL POST OFFICE, ADELAIDE.

CHAPTER VI.

SOUTH AUSTRALIA.

CONFIGURATION—THE LAKE COUNTRY—HEAT IN SUMMER—FRUIT—GLENELG—ADELAIDE—MOUNT LOFTY RANGE—PARKS AND BUILDINGS—MOSQUITO PLAIN CAVES—CAMELS—THE OVERLAND TELEGRAPH LINE—PEAKE STATION—THE NORTHERN TERRITORY—EARLY MISFORTUNES—PRESENT PROSPECTS—INSECT LIFE—ALLIGATORS—BUFFALOES.

SOUTH AUSTRALIA should rather be called Central Australia, for it lies half-way between the western and the eastern seaboard, and the colony runs right through the continent from north to south. It is an enormous tract, 2,000 miles in length and 700 in breadth. The total area is 903,000 square miles, of which at present barely a tenth is in occupation, though exploration has already made known the existence of millions of acres of magnificent pasture-land ready for settlement. In the colonies, when you speak of South Australia, you are understood to mean the district of which Adelaide is the centre. If you referred to the inland portion, you would speak of the 'far north;' and again, if you meant the Port Darwin—Gulf of Carpentaria country—you would use the term 'Northern Territory.' The original South Australia is first to be noticed.

No part of Australia is more strongly marked with Australian peculiarities than this. The Murray is the only river, and this stream brings down the waters of the ranges of the south-eastern colonies; the other streams are merely courses in which, under favourable conditions, water may be looked for,

WATERFALL GULLY, SOUTH AUSTRALIA.

and not otherwise. The ranges are few in number, and are of no great elevation. But the grass plains and the scrub plains are immense. Gazing round from an eminence, the impression produced by the equal height of the vegetation, and the dull glaucous colour of the foliage, is that you are looking upon the open rolling illimitable ocean. South Australia contains whole principalities of the ordinary park-like bush of Australia; the eucalypts standing in grass without any undergrowth, either singly or in clumps, as though planted by a landscape gardener. If an expert were whisked during his sleep—like another Bedreddin Hassan—and dropped from Europe, Asia,

Africa or America anywhere in these regions, he would exclaim the moment he opened his eyes—''Tis Australia.' A glance at the map would lead to the conclusion that the colony is well supplied with lakes. On paper, Lake Torrens, Lake Eyre, Lake Gardiner, Lake Amadeus, cover large areas, but unfortunately an antipodean meaning must be attached to the term; for the most part these lakes are either muddy reed-covered swamps, or salt marshes unfitted for navigation in winter, and evaporating into vast glittering clay pans in summer. The level of several of these extensive depressions is believed to

A MURRAY RIVER BOAT.

be below that of the sea, and the cutting of a canal to unite them to Spencer's Gulf, the deepest indentation on the southern coast, has been suggested, and will probably some day be carried into effect, and then there may be changes worked in the climate.

At present, however, South Australia is decidedly hot during its summer months of December, January and February. The thermometer runs up to 110 and 112 and 116 degrees. 'But then,' says the typical South Australian, taking you by the buttonhole, 'it is a dry heat, and really you do not feel it; there is no enervating aqueous vapour about;' and there certainly is not.

No complaints of wet and sloppy weather are ever to be heard. On the contrary, when the south-easter brings a heavy bursting bank of cloud with it, there is a general rubbing of hands and utterance of congratulatory remarks. 'Splendid rain to-day,' is the usual phrase; and 'How far north does it extend?' is the current query. But, admitting that the South Australian summer is hot, it must be added that the climate during the other eight months is delightful. One enthusiast declares that the pure soft balmy air is such as one would expect to blow over 'the plains of heaven;' and at any rate there is first-class medical testimony that for people with weak lungs there are few more

ADELAIDE IN 1837.

hopeful resorts. The 'far north' is subject to droughts and to floods, and the Northern Territory has a weather system of its own. As the description of its climate suggests, South Australia is a grand fruit country. Grapes, peaches, apricots and oranges, grow practically without cultivation, and attain perfection in the open air. In the season there are few tables in Adelaide on which piles of grapes and plates of apricots and peaches are not to be regularly found. The fruit can be purchased in the market at a penny a pound, so that at current wages there is no occasion for the poorest of the working classes to stint in these luscious products of the soil.

Adelaide, the metropolis of South Australia, called after the wife of William IV., was founded in 1836. To-day, with its suburbs, it contains about 170,000 inhabitants. On the 28th of December, 1836, Captain Hindmarsh, who had served under Nelson at the Nile, landed from H.M.S. Buffalo at Holdfast Bay, in St. Vincent's Gulf, and beneath the shade of a patriarchal gum-tree, and in presence of a few officials, read his commission as the first Governor of South Australia. The anniversary of that event is observed as a public holiday by all classes in the community, while the old gum-tree has become a source of solicitude, and is reverently cared for by the municipal authorities of Glenelg—a fashionable watering-place which has grown up within sight of Governor Hindmarsh's landing-place.

And indeed this Glenelg is a fitting entrance to the fair city of Adelaide, with which it is connected by two lines of railway. Facing the dazzling white beach are the seaside residences of squatting kings, wealthy merchants, and other successful colonists; while the bay itself is studded with yachts and other pleasure craft, with perchance a man-of-war, or two or three mail steamers, at anchor in the offing, for all the ocean-borne mails are either landed or shipped at Glenelg. During the summer evenings the sands and long jetty are thronged with visitors from the capital, who have come down to enjoy the fresh cool breezes, or to listen to the various bands of music.

Adelaide itself is laid out on a gently sloping ground, from 96 to 176 feet above the sea-level, on both sides of the Torrens, which is spanned by three large handsome bridges. The part out north is called North Adelaide, to distinguish it from 'the City,' which lies on the other side of the river. The streets are all unusually broad, even for Australian cities, and run at right angles, many of them being bordered with rows of trees, the shade of which is very refreshing in the hot summer days. One of the features of the place is the number and extent of its beautiful public squares and park lands. In this respect it transcends even Melbourne. The squares in each quarter of the city are reserves of several acres in extent, embellished with flowers, trees, and fountains; while the parks are extensive reservations, surrounding the city on every side, separating it from the suburbs.

Adelaide, with ordinary care, can never be other than a healthy city. Moreover, it can never extend its boundaries. This fact accounts for the high prices obtained for city property. Land originally bought for eight or ten shillings an acre has recently changed hands at £1000 a foot. Its surroundings are the charms of the city. On the west is the sea. Four or five miles to the east is the thickly wooded Mount Lofty range, so called from the highest peak, 2400 feet above the sea-level, which, trending away to the southward, closes in on that side the undulating plain on which the city is built. To the northward the range takes a more easterly direction for twenty or forty miles. These hills, which are reached from Adelaide by railways and tram-lines, and excellent carriage-roads, are a favourite summer resort of those citizens who can afford to avail themselves of the coolness and seclusion which they offer.

The buildings in Adelaide show well. A very white freestone has entered largely into the more recent erections; and, as there are comparatively few large factories in the city, and no shipping nearer than Port Adelaide, they lose but little of their pristine freshness by smoke and grime. Then the unpleasant effect produced by the sight of a hovel adjoining a palatial bank or pile of warehouses several storeys high, is of rare occurrence,

KING WILLIAM STREET, ADELAIDE.

while the broad streets offer the most advantageous conditions for the display of the various architectural styles employed. The town has been called 'the city of churches;' and the number of ecclesiastical edifices which it contains places its pretensions to that distinction beyond question. The Anglican Cathedral of St. Peter is a large and imposing building, a portion of which is still uncompleted, occupying an elevated position in the southern portion of North Adelaide. The Roman Catholic Cathedral of St. Francis

Xavier is in the south, and recalls the early days of the colony, when the prophecies of its future importance were few in number. All the other great religious bodies are also creditably represented.

Nearly all the Government departments are in the vicinity of Victoria Square, an ornamental reserve, through which King William Street, one of the most handsome thoroughfares in Australia, has been carried. No traveller should leave Adelaide without spending some hours in the Botanical Garden. To omit that lovely resort would be an error indeed.

AN ADELAIDE PUBLIC SCHOOL.

South Australia contains a little over 300,000 inhabitants. Its chief industries are agricultural, pastoral, and mining. Very early in its history it became the granary of the colonies, and, although it can no longer claim that distinction, it is still one of the few places in the world where the visitor can travel over three hundred miles in the same direction between fields of waving yellow corn. Despite the small returns from wheat-growing, the area under cultivation is enlarged every year, and is now not less than two million acres. More attention is being paid to scientific farming, thanks to the influence of the recently established Agricultural College at Roseworthy, thirty miles north of Adelaide, experimental farms in various parts of the colony, and the lectures delivered in the chief agricultural centres. The yield is so dependent on the rainfall that the average for the colony rarely exceeds ten bushels per acre, and occasionally falls below three. The subject of irrigation has lately been warmly taken up by the agricultural community, and the next few years will see not only a more rational system of farming, but the adoption of means to render that community less dependent on the uncertain rainfall. At the London Exhibition a splendid

REAPING IN SOUTH ADELAIDE.

sample of wheat grown at Mount Barker—a beautifully situated township amongst the hills, twenty miles south-east of Adelaide—obtained the highest award.

Of the show places of South Australia none are more interesting than the curious caves of the Mosquito Plains. They have been described at length by the naturalist Tennison Woods, in his *Geological Observations of South Australia*: 'In the midst of a sandy, swampy country, a series of caves is found, whose internal beauty is at strange variance with the wildness of the scenery around. The entrance is merely a round hole on the top of a hill, which leads to a small sloping path under a shelf of rock. Descending this for about twenty-five feet, one gets a first glimpse of the magnificence enshrined below. The observer finds himself at the entrance of a large oblong square chamber, low, but perfectly lighted by an aperture at the opposite end; and all around, above and below, the eye is bewildered by a profusion of ornaments and decorations of Nature's own devising. It resembles an immense Gothic cathedral, and the numbers of half-finished stalagmites, which rise from the ground like kneeling or prostrate forms, seem worshippers in that silent and solemn place. At the farther end is an immense stalactite, which appears like a support to the whole roof; not the least beautiful part of it being that it is tinted by almost every variety of colour, one side being of a delicate azure, with passages of blue, green, and pink intermingled; and again it is snowy white, finally merging into a golden yellow. The second cave or chamber is so thickly studded with stalactites that it seems like a carefully arranged scene, which, from the interminable variety of form and magic effect of light and shade, might easily be taken to represent some fairy palace. Very soon the cavern becomes as dark as night, and further exploration to the numerous chambers and fissures beyond has to be made by the assistance of torches. On leaving the last chamber, we return to the light; a narrow passage, richly wreathed with limestone, is observed on the right hand going out. Proceeding a little way down, a large vaulted chamber is reached, so perfectly dark and obscure that even torches can do but faint justice to its beauty. Here, above all other portions of the caves, has Nature been prodigal of the fantastic ornament with which the whole place abounds. There are pillars so finely formed, and covered with such delicate trellis-work, there are droppings of lime making such scroll-work, that the eye is bewildered with the extent and variety of the adornment. It is like a palace of ice with frozen cascades and fountains all round.'

A special feature of the settlers' life in the 'far north' is the increasing use of camels. At Beltana a camel-breeding establishment has been in existence for nearly twenty years. Sir Thomas Elder introduced the animals first from Afghanistan, and, as they are found to be well adapted for work in Central Australia, they are now largely used. They are broken in to draw drays, or to trot with a buggy behind them; and the 'belle of Beltana' uses one for a hack. Nearly a thousand camels have been provided from this establishment for hauling stores and for doing the every-day work of bullock and horses. The ordinary team is composed of six camels. A team of eight will drag a dray with three tons of goods through the heaviest sand. The animals wear large leather collars, and their harness is in other respects very similar to that used for horse teams. No great difficulty has been experienced in training the camel to this novel sort of work. But the Australian bushman would not hesitate about putting a hippopotamus into harness.

For pluck in public works South Australia has a character of her own. One of her great enterprises was the construction of the 'Overland Telegraph Line' from Adelaide on the one side to Port Darwin on the other side of the continent, to meet the cable laid from Singapore to that place, and thus to establish direct communication with Great Britain. Two years were spent in this arduous undertaking. The country was awkward; materials and stores had to be transported across the desert as the work went on. For months the parties were stopped by floods; some perished from thirst, and the blacks harassed others. When at last the line was up it was found that the white ants had destroyed the poles in the Northern Territory, and they had to be replaced with iron columns. One contractor and one officer after another gave up in despair, and at last Mr. Charles Todd, Superintendent of Telegraphs, who was responsible for the

CAMEL SCENES.

scheme, had to leave his city office; and, though he had no bush experience, his zeal and his intelligence were rewarded with success. An engraving is given on page 98 of Mr. Todd and three of his most energetic colleagues in the work: Messrs. Paterson, Mitchell, and Little. The work was begun in 1870, and on August 22, 1872, the first message was sent over the 1700 miles of wire. It was feared that the blacks would never let the line stand, but, though they have 'stuck up' the stations occasionally and killed operators, they have never interfered with the wires. While the line was being constructed the operators gave every black who visited them the opportunity of enjoying a gratuitous electric shock. The peculiar sensation vividly affected their nerves and their imagination, and thus a wholesome awe was engendered of what they called 'the white-fellow's devil.' The illustration given on this page represents Peake Telegraph Station, situated over seven hundred miles north of Adelaide. The large building in the centre is the telegraph station and Government buildings; to the right is a cattle station. The hills in the background are mostly of a stony character common to Central Australia, with a slight

PEAKE OVERLAND TELEGRAPH STATION.

growth of bushes here and there. Round about the station there are large numbers of blacks camped, and the officers have to go about heavily armed. The station at Barrow Creek, farther north, was 'stuck up' by the blacks a few years ago, and two of the officers killed. At every station there are usually two operators and four line repairers. As the adjacent station is 150 or 200 miles away, and there are no nearer neighbours, the little garrisons lead a lonely life. Whenever a breakage occurs two men start from either station between which the fault exists; each party takes, besides a supply of wire, a field instrument, and at every thirty miles a 'shackle' is put down, and the party communicates with its own station, and so each proceeds until one or the other finds and repairs the defect. Communication being restored, the news is conveyed to the other party, and both take up their instruments and retrace their steps without having seen each other.

At the Barrow Creek station, a party of the employés were surprised in 1875 by the blacks, when they had left the building to indulge in a bathe. They had to run for their lives through a volley of spears to regain the shelter of their loop-holed home. Mr. Stapleton and a line repairer were mortally wounded, and two others were badly hurt. Mr. Stapleton was found to be sinking rapidly. The news was flashed to Adelaide. In one room of the city stood the doctor and Mrs. Stapleton, listening to the 'click, click' of the messages. A thousand miles away in the desert, in a lonely hut beleaguered by the blacks, lay the dying man with an instrument brought to his bedside. He received the doctor's message that his case was hopeless. He heard his wife's adieus, and he telegraphed an eternal farewell. It is easy to believe that the affecting spectacle moved those around the group in Adelaide to tears.

South Australia's next great feat is to run a railway across the continent. Already the line is completed a distance of nearly four hundred miles northwards towards Strangeways Springs. Camels imported by Mr. H. J. Scott are used to carry stores, rations and water to the men employed in advance, whilst, from the other end, the Palmerston and Pine Creek line, 150 miles in length, is in the hands of the contractors. It is hoped that within the next ten years the transcontinental railway will be completed, thereby uniting Australia and the east.

When John McDouall Stuart at last crossed the continent from sea to sea and from north to south, there was great enthusiasm in Adelaide. The explorer received £5000 from Parliament, and the colony obtained permission to push its bounds up to the Indian Ocean, thus annexing a nice little tract of 531,402 square miles. Thus, in the year 1863, was the Northern Territory acquired. It was resolved at once to form a settlement in the new country. The Imperial Government from time to time had endeavoured to colonise North Australia, settlements being formed in turn at Melville Island, Raffles Bay, and Port Essington; but each place in turn was abandoned. Undeterred by these failures, the South Australian authorities sold land, marked out a township, appointed an official staff, and invited colonisation. And then South Australia went through its painful experience. The owners of land warrants complained that they had been 'sold' as well as the land; the expected colonists did not put in an appearance; while the members of the staff were quarrelling, the blacks made a raid and stole and destroyed nearly all the stores, and finally many of the Government officers took to open boats and escaped after a hazardous sea voyage to Western Australia. For years and years the Northern Territory was a source of expense and anxiety to the good people of Adelaide; but a colonist—and least of all a South Australian colonist—never despairs. The party that counselled abandonment was looked upon with scorn, and after every disaster a new staff was sent up to Port Darwin, and more and more attractive land offers were made. But the Adelaide Government was taught the lesson all larger and more important Governments have yet to acquire : namely, that you cannot force colonisation, that the one condition of success is a natural growth. Times have changed recently. The overlanders, having accounted for Queensland, pushed into the Northern Territory, and conse-

COLLINGROVE STATION, SOUTH AUSTRALIA.

quent upon their favourable reports runs have been taken up in all directions, and in immense areas, and in all probability the Northern Territory is on the eve of a great development. In the last two or three years tens of thousands of cattle have been moved from Queensland and New South Wales into the new country, and at the Roper and Macarthy rivers bush townships have been established, and the town of Palmerston (Port Darwin) has witnessed a large increase in private and substantial buildings. Prospectors have opened up gold, copper and tin mines. The gold export is now £75,000 per annum, and copper mines are being energetically worked;

and a railway which is about to be constructed to the present mineral centre is expected to effect a revolution, as the want of carriage has hitherto checked mining progress.

Residents in the Northern Territory speak hopefully about the climate. That the white man cannot perform the same amount of constant work in tropical Australia that he can in his own climes and countries is admitted, but still, it is contended, he can work and be healthy and happy. There is an absence amongst the population of the enervation so conspicuous in India, Java,

SHEEP IN THE SHADE OF A GUM-TREE.

Singapore, and Ceylon. Artisans ply their callings on the eight hours system, as elsewhere in Australia, without special precautions against the sun. The climate is, in fact, more Australian than it is tropical. But at Port Darwin itself there is much to remind the traveller that he is in the tropics, and is nearer to the equator than to Capricorn. Mingled with the characteristic flora of Australia are the palms, bamboos, rattan canes, and wild nutmeg-trees, and other flora of the adjacent Spice Islands. The ground, the vegetation, and the atmosphere are alive with insect life. Linnaeus has eleven orders of insects, but, as one settler facetiously remarks, had the eminent naturalist in question visited the Northern Territory, he might have classified one hundred and eleven orders. Fire-flies flit about; beetles display their metallic brilliancy; radiant moths and butterflies fleck the gloom. The observant man admires and marvels; but not always does the view charm, for myriads of mosquitoes and sand-flies have at him, and the bung-fly, attacking the eyelid, will cause a swelling that will close up the eye for several days. Ants are found literally in legions. In the houses some amusement is to be derived from watching the ant-eating lizard, who is allowed to run up and down the walls without molestation, and is, indeed, welcomed as a highly useful domestic animal. In the bush surprise is excited by the enormous ant-hills. Some are twenty-five feet in height, and six or eight feet in diameter; but usually they are from six to twelve feet high, and about four feet in diameter; and along a belt of country extending perhaps one hundred miles, they may stand apart but fifty or a hundred feet. To level these cunningly devised cellular structures, occasionally, would prove far more costly than levelling the ground of timber. In other places the 'meridional' ant-hill is met with. These edifices are from three to six feet high, and more. They are broad at the base, and taper to a point at the summit. The form therefore is that of a long wedge, and the peculiarity is that all the summit lines are true north and south, as though laid down by a surveyor.

In the rivers the traveller is introduced to the alligator. Many are the tales of horror and of escape related in connection with these saurians. One member of the original exploring party of the South Australian Government, a man named Reid, fell asleep in a boat on the Roper river, with his leg hanging carelessly over the side of the craft. An alligator seized the limb and dragged the man out of the boat, his screams too late calling attention to his fate. The alligator is found right down the Queensland coast. While writing, the following telegram appears in the *Argus* (Melbourne, March 10, 1886): 'A girl named Margaret Gordon, the daughter of a dairyman on Cattle Creek, thirty miles from Townsville, has been devoured by an alligator. She went with a servant-girl to the creek for water, when a large alligator rushed at her and carried her off. The occurrence was witnessed by the girl's father, who was unable to render any assistance.'

The one trace left of the early settlements of Raffles Bay and Port Essington is that herds of buffaloes are to be met with in the districts in question, and also some Timor ponies. Both animals were introduced from Timor, and when the settlements were abandoned males and females were left to run wild. The buffaloes have spread along the north coast, nearly, if not quite, to the Gulf of Carpentaria, and to the south as far as the bottom of Van Diemen's Gulf. They are generally found congregated in herds of twenty to fifty, under the guidance of a single full-grown male, oftentimes of enormous size. But stragglers are often met with far beyond these limits. The young males are turned out of the herd by the patriarch as soon as

they approach maturity, becoming wanderers for life unless they can re-
establish themselves, or gain a footing in other herds; and this can only be
done by killing or driving off the leading bull. Of course many are doomed
to a solitary life, and roam far from the haunts of their fellows. There is
no danger of the buffaloes mixing with the herds of the settlers, as the
antagonism between these cattle races is pronounced and insurmountable.

THE BOTANICAL GARDENS, ADELAIDE.

QUEENSLAND.

BRISBANE.

A VILLAGE ON DARLING DOWNS.

CHAPTER VII.

QUEENSLAND.

SIZE AND CONFIGURATION—EARLY SETTLEMENT—BRISBANE ISLAND AND COAST TOWNS—GLADSTONE—ROMA—GYMPIE—TOOWOOMBA—TOWNSVILLE—COOKTOWN—SQUATTING—THE CATTLE STATION—THE SHEEP STATION—THE QUEENSLAND FOREST—THE NETTLE-TREE—SUGAR PLANTING—POLYNESIAN NATIVES—STOPPAGE OF THE LABOUR TRADE—GOLD MINING—THE PALMER—SILVER, TIN, AND COPPER.

THE following sketch of the great colony of Queensland is from the pen of Mr. Carl A. Feilberg of Brisbane.

In order to form a just idea of Queensland it is necessary to bear in mind the broad divisions of its territory. First, there is the coast country, which is often spoken of as a strip, though in reality it has at some points a depth of over two hundred miles. A glance at the map will show innumerable rivers finding their way into the sea along the whole east and north coasts of the colony, and it is the country which forms the watersheds of these rivers which is spoken of as the coast. West and south of this bordering tract lies the great central plateau, which is mainly a huge plain, where the surface, which sometimes rises into rolling downs and sometimes spreads out in apparently limitless flats, is only broken by a few ranges of low hills. From this great plateau the whole surface drainage is to the south and south-west, a small portion finding its way into the Darling, but the greater part flowing by a network of channels through the thirsty sands which lie to the north of the lakes, or more properly the huge swamps of South Australia. In the coast country the rainfall in ordinary seasons is sufficient in quantity and sufficiently spread over the year to permit of agriculture. The rivers and creeks generally contain running streams of water, and the air is moist enough to permit the fall of dew at night. In the interior the rivers are watercourses that seldom contain running streams, being during the greater part of the year merely chains of pools, or 'water holes,' as they are locally called. Rain falls at long and uncertain intervals: the annual total is small; night-dews are not common, and agriculture is virtually impossible unless assisted by irrigation. To this general description there is, however, one important exception. In the southern part of the colony the table-land approaches to within seventy or eighty miles of the seaboard, and therefore enjoys a comparatively moist climate. The district so situated, known as the Darling Downs, lies immediately to the west of Brisbane, and is the seat of the most important agricultural settlement of the colony. The moister climate of the Darling Downs changes almost imperceptibly as they stretch to the westward, and it is difficult to fix on the point where agriculture, carried on in the usual way, without irrigation, may be regarded as a hopeless task.

The occupation of the territory now included in Queensland began almost simultaneously at two points. Pioneer squatters, pushing northward from the interior of New South Wales, discovered the fertile plains of the Darling Downs, and the Sydney authorities determined to form a convict station on the shores of the remote almost unexplored sheet of land-locked water known as Moreton Bay. The convict station was founded in 1826, and in the first instance on the coast at a place since known as Humpy Bong, meaning, in the language of the blacks, 'dead huts or houses.' This settlement was soon abandoned, as the water-supply was precarious, and there was insufficient shelter for shipping. A site was subsequently chosen about twenty miles up the channel of the principal river emptying into Moreton Bay, which had been named after Sir Thomas Brisbane; and 'The Settlement,' as it was at first called, soon came to be known by the name of the river, and the decaying buildings of the first attempted lodgment caused the wandering blacks to give the locality the name it now bears.

At first, of course, there were nothing but the necessary buildings for the convicts—dangerous characters who had been convicted for fresh crimes in the land of their exile, and were therefore relegated to what was then the safe isolation of Moreton Bay—and for the warders and others in charge of the prisoners. Meanwhile, as we have said, pioneer squatters had spied out the pastoral wealth of the Darling Downs, and some bold adventurers had pushed overland with their flocks to occupy it. These pioneers at first kept up communication by bush trails with far distant Sydney, but, hearing that a new settlement had been formed on the coast, they sought to open communication with it. A pass—known as Cunningham's Gap—was found in 1832 through the ranges which form the eastern flanks of the great plateau, and communication was opened with the settlement. Townships were formed. Near the verge of the Darling Downs plateau the seed of what is now the thriving and important town of Toowoomba was sown by the carriers making a halting-place before attempting the toilsome and dangerous descent through the ravines of the thickly wooded range, which then swarmed with bold and hostile savages. Another such halting-place was the spot where travellers, having emerged from the broken country and having passed the great scrubs or jungles at the foot of the hills—now a populated and thriving farming district—first struck the navigable waters of the Bremer, the principal affluent of the Brisbane. At that point the town of Ipswich came into existence, and for many years it rivalled Brisbane in importance, because the goods brought to the capital by sea-going ships were taken in river craft to the former town, which was thus the point of departure for all land carriage.

Brisbane grew slowly. There was no special attraction to induce people to leave the more populated districts of New South Wales, and bury themselves in so remote a settlement. There was the fever which attacks settlers in all newly opened settlements, the blacks were dangerous, and that the place was a station for doubly and trebly convicted felons told against it. But the rich Darling Downs came to be regarded as a pastoral paradise, and squatting occupation spread rapidly in the interior, so that its expansion told slowly but surely on the outpost. The convict establishment was in time closed. The plot of ground formerly cultivated by the convicts is now occupied partly by a fine public garden, and partly by the domain surrounding the Governor's residence.

Brisbane is a fast-growing city, with a population, including the suburbs, of between 50,000 and 60,000, its growth since the census of 1881 having been so rapid that it is not possible to furnish more than an approximate estimate of the number. Originally built on a flat, partly enclosed by an abrupt bend of the river, the town has climbed the bordering ridges, crossed the stream and spread out in all directions. The principal street—Queen Street—runs across the neck of the original river-side 'pocket;' at one end it touches the wharves, at the other it meets the winding river at right angles, and the roadway is carried on by a long iron bridge across to the important suburb of South Brisbane. Queen Street, which is the combined Collins and Bourke Streets of Brisbane, promises to be a fine-looking thoroughfare. Already it possesses shops and bank buildings which may challenge comparison with those of any Australian city, and every year the older buildings are giving way to new and more imposing structures. On one side of the thoroughfare the cross-streets lead through the oldest part of the city; through blocks of buildings where fine warehouses and tumbledown hovels are strangely intermixed with the Parliament Houses, the public gardens, and the wharves. On the other side of Queen Street the same cross-streets climb steep ridges to the terraces, where high and broken ground offer cool breezy sites for streets filled with dwelling-houses.

The diversified surface of the ground over which the town of Brisbane has spread itself, the broad noble river which winds through it, doubling back almost on itself, as if loth to quit the city it has called into existence, and the picturesque range of wooded hills which closes the view to the westward,

VALLEY OF THE RIVER BRISBANE, QUEENSLAND.

constitute a scene of great beauty. An artist roaming round the town would find objects of interest everywhere. From the elevated terraces he could look down on the main town, with the river, a broad band of silver, winding through it, and his horizon would include the blue peaks of the main range to the westward, and the shimmer of the sunlight on the great landlocked sheet of Moreton Bay to the eastward.

One of the sights of Brisbane is the Garden of the Acclimatisation Society —a body supported partly by private subscription and partly by Government endowment. In these Gardens are collected a vast number of trees and plants selected for their use and beauty, and the sub-tropical position of Brisbane allows the propagation of the vegetable products of almost every zone. The 'bush house' in these gardens, a huge structure consisting of a rough framework roofed with dried bushes, covers several acres, and is stocked with a most interesting collection of ferns, lycopods, orchids, dracænas, colans, begonias, &c. There is a public museum, which is well stocked, and its specimens of natural history are well arranged.

The use of timber for buildings is very general in Brisbane. Pine is abundant on the coast of Queensland, and the easily worked timber is cheap. The climate is very mild, and their weatherboard walls are quite sufficient to keep out the very moderate cold experienced in winter; almost all the dwelling-houses, and many of the stores in the suburbs, are therefore wooden buildings. The dwelling-houses also are nearly all detached, standing each one in an allotment of its own, so that the residential part of the town straggles over an immense area, stretching out in fragmentary streets for miles from the main city. There are hundreds of neat cottages and trim villas scattered over the low hills and valleys, on the river bank, or nestling under the range of hills which lie to the west of the town. It should be remembered, however, that in the climate of Brisbane the 'verandah is the best room in the house,' and people live as much as possible in the open air; the family group gathers on the verandah in the evening instead of, as in a colder climate, congregating indoors.

The extended coast-line of Queensland, and the peculiar position of Brisbane in the extreme south, has prevented it from concentrating the social and commercial life of the colony, as is done by Sydney, Melbourne and Adelaide. It is by far the largest coast town, the centre of government, and its commerce is larger than that of all the remaining ports put together, but these ports are many of them also real capitals and commercial cities. The first important town on the coast going northward is Maryborough, on the banks of the Mary River, a town containing probably 10,000 inhabitants, and the commercial capital of a rich agricultural and mineral district, of somewhat limited extent. Maryborough disputes with Brisbane the possession of the most extensive ironworks in the colony, the demand for sugar and mining machinery having called them into existence. Rockhampton, near the mouth of the Fitzroy, is a town of equal if not greater population than Maryborough, but it is a far finer and better built city. Being the west terminus of the central system of trunk railways, it is essentially a commercial capital, and a busy, thriving place. Agricultural operations are not as yet very extensively carried on in the surrounding district, neither sugar-growing nor general cultivation having at present helped to increase the prosperity of Maryborough, nor is there any successful gold-field in the vicinity, though one phenomenally rich mine, Mount Morgan, is being worked in the neighbourhood. Rockhampton has grown and prospered by trade, and as it is the outlet for over 100,000 square miles of territory, it should have a very prosperous career before it.

The towns named are the most important on the coast-line of sub-tropical Queensland. There are also the thriving little towns of Bundaberg, at the mouth of the Burnett river, the outlet for a rich tract of agricultural land, and Gladstone, a few miles to the south of the mouth of the Fitzroy. The last-named township is next after Brisbane the oldest settlement in Queensland, but it has never prospered. Hidden away at the head of a great land-locked sheet of deep water—probably after Sydney the finest natural harbour on the east coast of Australia—it slumbers peacefully without any visible trade: a bush village, supported by the stockmen employed on the neighbouring cattle stations, and occasionally galvanised into life by a promising discovery among the rich but fragmentary and erratic mineral lodes found in the volcanic country in its vicinity. These constitute all the coast towns worth mentioning.

Inland, on the line of trunk railway running westward from Brisbane, are Ipswich and Toowoomba, both agricultural centres, but the latter the more important of the two, with a population of eight or nine thousand people. Just beyond Toowoomba, a branch of the railway curving to the south runs to Warwick, another pretty country town of some four thousand people, surrounded by rich soil and thriving farmers, and enjoying, from its elevation, a pleasantly cool climate. Continuing, the branch railway reaches Stanthorpe, near the border, mentioned elsewhere, and the line is being continued to effect a junction with the New South Wales railway system. After leaving Toowoomba, the main line continues in a nearly direct line westward, passing through Dalby, a rather stagnant little bush town of some two thousand people, set down in the midst of vast plains more suited by reason of the climate for pasture than agriculture. These plains may be regarded as the limit of the Darling Downs. Beyond them the railway runs through a desolate tract of scrub—not the fertile jungle of the coast districts, but an arid tract closely filled with stunted trees, hard and gnarled by their long struggle for existence. Emerging from this belt, the railway reaches another open tract, consisting of the true pastoral downs country, and runs into the pleasant little town of Roma, where from three to four thousand persons find employment in supplying the wants of the surrounding pastoral region. Still continuing, the railway is being pushed on westward towards the great pastoral area of the interior—the fertile wilderness which Burke and Wills first traversed, and where they died, which now is being filled by millions of sheep, and adding rapidly to the wealth of the colony. There are bush townships in the track of the advancing railway which will no doubt become towns, but as yet they are in no way noticeable. The same may be said of the townships reached by the Central Trunk Railway running westward from Rockhampton and its branches. The country through which it runs has not a climate very suitable for agriculture—at least no agricultural settlement has taken place—and with the exception of Clermont, a little town of about two thousand inhabitants, which grew into some importance by means of mineral discoveries in its vicinity, there are only bush townships of varying sizes in the central districts. The thriving town of Gympie, with five thousand inhabitants, the second gold-field of Queensland, and also the centre of a thriving and spreading agricultural settlement, lies about seventy miles to the south of Maryborough, with which it is connected by railway.

The line of the Tropic of Capricorn runs close to the town of Rockhampton ; sub-tropical Queensland ends there. The first place of importance on the coast going north is Mackay, a town of some three or four thousand people, supported by a small rich district which has become the chief centre of sugar cultivation in the colony. The Mackay district is in a sense isolated, having little or no trade connection with the interior. Next after Mackay comes Bowen, a sleepy, decaying settlement of some one thousand inhabitants, occupying a most beautiful site on a sheet of water land-locked by a ring of picturesque islands. There is no prettier town on the coast of Queensland, no place which seems more fitted for the site of a great city than Bowen ; but trade left it soon after its foundation, and it has mouldered half-forgotten ever since.

From Bowen northward the coast of Queensland is sheltered by the line of the Barrier Reef and a long chain of romantic and beautiful islands. The traveller on this coast enjoys a perpetual feast of the eye. On the one side the islands in the line of reef present every variety of form and colour—the green of the timber or vegetation clothing them, the varying lines of their fantastic, weather-beaten, rocky cliffs, and the dazzling white coral sand of their beaches. On the other side, the mountains of the coast range approach closely to the shore, sometimes apparently springing upwards from the very beach; and their imposing masses, clothed with dense vegetation to the very summits, smile rather than frown on the blue sparkling wavelets of the sheltered water, which seems to lave their feet. At various points the mountains fall back, opening, as it were, avenues to the interior of the country. At the entrance to one of these openings is Townsville, the chief commercial centre and the virtual capital of the north. This fast-growing city is built on the actual sea-coast ; and though to some extent sheltered by islands, its harbour is shallow and exposed. A breakwater, however, is being gradually made, and in various ways an artificial harbour is being formed. Townsville, which now contains probably a population of nine or ten thousand people, is the terminus of the Northern Trunk line. Immediately to the west of it are the great gold-fields of Charters Towers and Ravenswood, and the railway is being pushed far to the westward, traversing the northern portion of the pastoral plateau of the west, and tapping the verge of the great plains which slope gradually to the shore of the Gulf of Carpentaria. Townsville promises to be a very fine city; and, although it is too new a settlement to contain many buildings of special note, it will not long be without them.

Still following the coast, and passing the little mountain-bound port of Cardwell, which nestles at the feet of great hills which, by cutting it off from inland traffic, have stunted its growth, and by the ports of Cairns and Port Douglas, which dispute between them the lucrative position of outlet for the mineral fields on the elevated mountain plateau lying just behind them, we come to Cooktown. This town, built at the mouth of the Endeavour River, on the spot where Captain Cook careened his vessel after the discovery of Australia, was called into existence by the great gold rush of the Palmer, described elsewhere. Its fortunes waxed with the rush, and waned as the

TOWNSVILLE, NORTH QUEENSLAND.

alluvial field became exhausted; so that its population, Chinese and European, is now probably not more than two thousand souls. There is, however, a future before it, because a railway, now in course of construction, will soon link it with the Palmer gold-field, where there are hundreds of gold-reefs awaiting cheaper carriage and more certain communication with the coast for their full development. In the meantime Cooktown is becoming a centre for the nascent New Guinea trade, and a certain amount of settlement is taking place in its vicinity. This is the best port on the mainland of the Cape York peninsula, but at its extremity there is the port of Thursday Island, a shipping centre, and the northern outpost of Australia. At Thursday Island there is a Government resident, charged with the control of the pearling fleet, which has its head-quarters there, and the government of the scattered islands in Torres Straits, which are under the jurisdiction of Queensland. Thursday Island is a port of call for all vessels passing through Torres Straits, and several thousand tons of coal are always stored there.

On the Gulf of Carpentaria are two small ports. The principal one, Normanton, on the Norman River, is a growing town of over a thousand inhabitants, and will probably be the terminus of a line of railway. Burketown, on the Albert River, is a place which is reviving after a strange history. About twenty years ago, when the pioneer squatters first drove their herds into the Gulf country, a township was located there; but the settlers formed their settlement and lived in such reckless defiance of all sanitary rules that a fatal fever broke out, which decimated them. The place was after this entirely abandoned, and the grass hid the rotting posts of the mouldering houses, which rapidly decayed in that hot, moist climate. A few years ago, however, the attempt to form a town was renewed, and this time with more care. Burketown is now quite as healthy as any tropical settlement; and as it is surrounded by vast plains of exceptional fertility, abundantly watered by flowing streams, it will probably become a place of some importance. This completes the list of towns on the coast of Northern Queensland.

Queensland is pre-eminently the cattle colony, possessing no less than 4,266,172 head of horned stock in 1884. Experience has shown that sheep do not thrive in the coast districts, especially in the north. The merino breed of sheep will thrive, in spite of an exceedingly high summer temperature, provided the heat is dry, but not when the warmth is accompanied by moisture; so that in Queensland sheep-raising is practically confined to the table-lands of the interior. Cattle, on the other hand, do as well on the short scanty grasses, and in the dry pure air of the uplands, as on the rank luxuriant herbage and in the steamy atmosphere of the great plains which lie sweltering in the sun round the shores of the Gulf of Carpentaria. The whole colony is therefore available for cattle, while probably not more than half, or at the utmost two-thirds, can be used by the sheep-grazier. It is not possible, however, to lay down any definite boundaries between the sheep and cattle countries, because at many points the one melts insensibly into the other, and prolonged experience is sometimes required to fix the dividing line with any degree of accuracy.

The sheep-owner comes when the wilderness has been partly subdued, the blacks tamed and reduced to idle drunken loafers, and the facilities and cost of carriage greatly reduced. He must either be a capitalist or have the command of large sums of money, for he has to subdivide his country with great paddocks inclosed by wire fences; he must supplement the natural stores of water by scooping out reservoirs, sinking wells, or damming creek channels; and he must erect costly buildings as wool-sheds, stores, huts, &c. The term squatter is quite misapplied to the wool kings of the present day, who are here men of business, watching the markets and the seasons, eager to utilise to its utmost every crop of grass which a good rain yields, and to turn it into mutton and wool, and buying and selling stock so as to profit by every turn of the market.

A good deal of the sheep farming of the colony is now carried on not by individuals, but by joint-stock companies with capitals of many hundred thousands of pounds. In fact, the old-time squatter—the type depicted in such books as Henry Kingsley's stories—is as extinct as the dodo in Queensland, so far as the sheep districts are concerned.

The cultivation of cereals and crops such as are grown in the southern colonies is only practised in Queensland on a considerable scale in the district of Darling Downs, where the comparatively cool climate of the inland plateau is accompanied by a sufficient rainfall to permit of ordinary farming. Wheat is grown, but not to any great extent, the total area under wheat in 1884 being less than 16,000 acres. The soil is very fertile, and the yield of grain per acre is decidedly above the Australian average; but for some reason red rust is a perfect scourge to the farmer.

It is on the fertile scrub land that the most successful agriculture is carried on. These scrubs are generally found on the banks of rivers, although in certain localities broad areas, containing hundreds of square miles, are clothed with scrub. The soil is a deep alluvial deposit; and the close-growing trees on it spring straight and tall in the struggle to reach the upper atmosphere and light, for the leafy roof allows no sun to penetrate to the damp ground, soft with mouldering leaves, but makes a cool green gloom even on the most fiery summer day. There is something very solemn in the quietude of a scrub untouched by the axe of the lumberer or settler. There is no undergrowth, properly speaking, though delicate little ferns and fairy-like mosses nestle close to the feet of the trees. But there is a wealth of parasitical life. Giant lianas twine from tree to tree, hanging in great loops and folds and contortions, suggesting the idea of huge vegetable monsters writhing in agony. Much more graceful are the lovely shy orchids hiding in crannies, and the bolder ferns, springing from great root-masses attached to the stems of the trees, the graceful shape and curve of the leaves, and their pure pale-green colour, undisturbed and un-dimmed by wind or sun. Among the wilderness of trees may be noticed the victims of the treacherous fig, the dead trunk of the original tree still visible, but enveloped in the interlacing stem of the robber, which has seized it in its cruel embrace, sucked life and marrow out of it, and reared triumphantly its crown of glossy green leaves far above in the bright sunlight. On all these beautiful or strange or weird objects one gazes in a stillness which seems to be intensified by the continuous murmur of the breeze in the leafy roof—a quiet so great that one is almost startled by the timid thud of the tiny scrub marsupial, which, after a gaze of fascinated terror at the intruder, hurries away, or by the clatter of a scrub pigeon or turkey far up in the overarching foliage, or the strange snoring call of the Australian sloth, or native bear.

In the tropical scrub the lianas, the creeping canes and creepers of every description, bind the trees into compact masses of vegetation; and it is a vegetation which, if one may be allowed the term, is of a fiercer type than in the south. Every creeper seems to be armed with thorns, to tear the clothes and lacerate the flesh of the rash intruder, and poisonous and stinging plants abound. Chief among these must be placed the nettle-tree, a shrub with broad green, soft-looking leaves, covered with a down that carries torture in every tiny fibre. Even horses brushed by these treacherous leaves

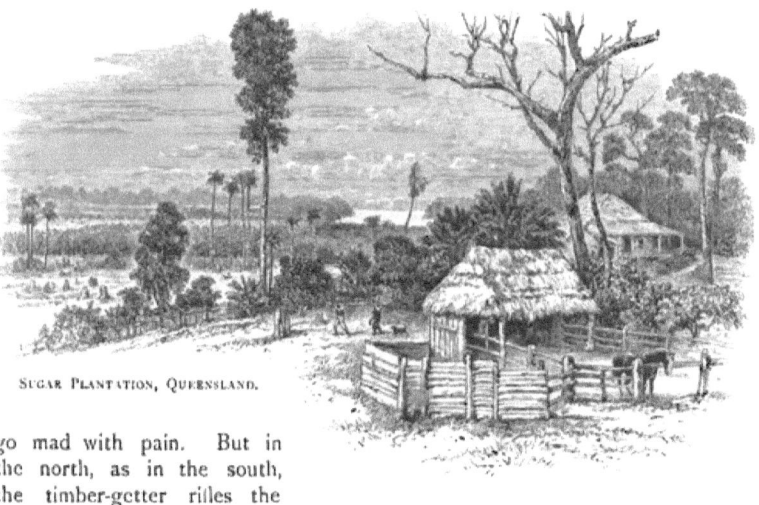

SUGAR PLANTATION, QUEENSLAND.

go mad with pain. But in the north, as in the south, the timber-getter rifles the scrub of its treasures of timber, and the sugar planter clears all before him, and skims with his cane-crops the incalculable store of fertility accumulated in the soil.

It is in connection with sugar-growing that the labour difficulty, common in Australia, becomes unusually severe in Queensland. The difficulty is two-fold—climatic and economical. Field work in the tropics is everywhere shunned by white men, and in Queensland, north of Mackay, it has not as yet been found possible to induce Europeans to engage in it. Some of the work connected with cane-growing, also, is peculiarly exhausting, because the canes, when they reach a height of six or seven feet, shut out every breeze, and the heat between the rows is stifling. Then a large staff of labourers is required on a plantation, because during the planter's harvest—the crushing season, which extends over some months—a considerable number of additional hands are required. In a colony where labour is well paid and work abundant there is practically no floating population to furnish these temporary supplies. It follows therefore that the planter must keep all the year round a staff equal to his harvest requirements, and the expense of doing this, if the men employed were paid at the high rate of wages current for white men, would be crushing. The difficulty has been, up to the present time, solved by the importation of South Sea Islanders, who are generally speaking good and docile labourers, not affected by heat, and comparatively cheap. They are engaged for terms of three years, at a wage in cash of £6 a year; but their employers have to feed and clothe them, and to pay for the cost of their introduction and their return to their homes when the engagements are terminated. It is reckoned that the cost of Kanaka labourers, including everything, equals from £25 to £35 a year for each 'boy' employed, though that of course is very much less than the £1 a week, with food and lodging, generally paid to white labourers.

The labour trade, as the procuring of Kanakas is termed, is, however, to be stopped in 1890. In spite of rigid regulations and the care exercised by the Government of the colony, it is a trade which, from its very nature, is liable to abuse, and it has been abused. Vessels trading to islands where the natives knew nothing of the colony or of regular work endeavoured by fraud and misrepresentation, and sometimes, though rarely, by actual violence to procure cargoes of labourers. It must be remembered that the Queensland labour trade has been ever since its establishment the bone of contention in fierce party disputes, and the usual unscrupulousness of party politicians has been displayed alike in attacking and defending it.

Taking a general view of agriculture, it must be admitted that Queenslanders have not, except in regard to sugar, taken advantage of their great opportunities. Sugar-growing, until the recent crisis in the labour difficulty, was progressing rapidly. The yield for 1885, though not officially stated, is computed by reliable experts at 50,000 tons of sugar, which is nearly all of a high quality, and worth probably about a million sterling. The wheat yield, as has been seen, is insignificant, and even of maize—which grows freely in every part of the colony—there is not enough produced to supply home consumption. In the tropical coast districts some attention is being paid to the cultivation of fruit for export. Pine-apples and bananas grow luxuriantly in all parts of the colony, but in the north they attain great size and develop a very fine flavour. These fruits, with mangoes, are now sent south in yearly increasing quantities. Arrowroot growing and manufacture is spreading in the districts round Brisbane, where the soil and climate seem to be especially suitable to the tuber. Coffee has been grown experimentally at several points on the coast, but nowhere in quantity, though the experiments have been highly successful. Cotton growing, which at one time was vigorously fostered by the Government in the southern coast districts, flourished so long as a bonus was paid on every bale exported, but when that support was withdrawn it was killed by the labour difficulty. Olives, almonds, figs, and fruits especially suited to a sub-tropical climate flourish in the same southern coast districts, but no attempt has been made to cultivate them on a commercial scale. An effort was made to establish silk production, and it resulted in the production of just enough silk to secure the promised bonus, and there the industry stopped. In fact, agriculture throughout the colony is crippled by its very prosperity. The high rate of wages prevalent, and the demand for labour in other fields, precludes the possibility of pursuing any agricultural industry which requires many hands, unless the product is exceptionally high-priced.

The mineral wealth of Queensland is surprising. Its gold-fields are of vast extent, and as yet hardly touched. There are innumerable copper lodes; stream and lode tin are being successfully worked; silver ores abound, and are being mined now; iron has been found in great quantities; extensive coal-fields exist, and are being worked in the vicinity of Brisbane and Maryborough; lead, nickel, cobalt, and bismuth ores have been found. The gold prospectors found their way to Queensland soon after the great alluvial fields of the south began to show signs of exhaustion, but for many years they found little to reward their efforts. There was, however, a prevailing idea among regular gold-miners—who, very soon after the first discoveries, began to form a distinct class in the population—that rich finds would be made in the northern colony. This belief led to the Canoona 'rush' in 1858, probably the most remarkable wild-goose chase in which the excitable Australian miners ever engaged. There was a report that gold had been found near the shores of Keppel Bay, then occupied only by a few cattle stations, and at once all the miners of Australia became excited. Steamers and sailing vessels, filled with eager men, discharged their living freights on the desolate shore, and in an incredibly short space of time many thousands of miners, scantily provided with the necessaries of life, had ascertained that the rush was a 'duffer'—that there was no gold—and were spreading over the face of the country, prospecting it in all directions. They found no gold, and were reduced to such straits that the Government of New South Wales, which then included Queensland, was compelled to charter craft to carry them away. But if they found no gold, they discovered and made known the value of the country, and laid the foundation of what is now the thriving town of Rockhampton. Gold was found in sufficient quantities to repay mining at Peak Downs, about two hundred miles inland from Rockhampton, where, it may be mentioned, the proprietors discovered a wonderfully rich lode of copper ore that was afterwards mined and produced many thousand tons of metal.

The gold yield of Queensland, however, for many years after separation was only trifling. In 1860 the whole gold export of the colony was only 4127 ounces, and in 1862 it sunk to 189 ounces. But in 1868 a prospector named Nash, travelling through the broken hilly country which forms the upper watershed of Mary River, found 'prospects' in a gully, which induced him to stay and try it. In a few days he rode into the sleepy seaport of Maryborough—then a stagnant township with grass-grown streets—and startled it by applying for a prospector's claim. In a few weeks the colony rang with the news that a really rich alluvial gold-field had been found, and in a few months from twelve to fifteen thousand people had congregated in the field of Gympie. It was a very rich but a limited field, and, though other neighbouring patches were opened out and worked, the alluvial deposits were soon exhausted. But there was better than alluvial gold at Gympie. The ridges were seamed with quartz reefs, which were proved to be richly impregnated with metal; and the gold yield from these reefs has been constant and increasing ever since. In 1884 Gympie yielded 112,051 ounces of gold, and it has given since it was first opened 1,043,131 ounces.

The last great gold discovery in Queensland was that of the Palmer in 1874. In the preceding year, Mr. (now Sir Arthur) Palmer, being Premier, sent out an exploring expedition to examine the unknown interior of the Cape York peninsula. In this report the explorers mentioned that they had found 'the colour' in the bed of a river which they named after the Premier. A party of four well-equipped northern miners acted on the hint. Carrying with them plenty of provisions and spare horses, they set out to examine the Palmer country, and soon found that the sand which overlays its rocky bed and the gullies running into it were impregnated with gold. A great rush ensued, and, though no very remarkable nuggets were discovered, and no specially rich finds were made, the gold was everywhere near the surface, and large quantities were unearthed. From its discovery to the end of 1884 the Palmer yielded 1,243,691 ounces.

WESTERN AUSTRALIA.

SHEEP-SHEARING.

PERTH.

CHAPTER VIII.

WESTERN AUSTRALIA.

EARLY SETTLEMENT — MISTAKEN LAND SYSTEM — CONVICT LABOUR — THE SYSTEM ABANDONED — POISON PLANTS — PERTH — KING GEORGE'S SOUND — CLIMATE — PEARLS — PROSPECTS.

WESTERN AUSTRALIA, as its name implies, is the tract of country lying upon the western side of the great island continent of the south. A glance at the map shows that the eastern side of the island, and much of the southern, is occupied by the colonies of South Australia, Victoria, New South Wales, and Queensland, the land in which is taken up by squatters, by agriculturists and miners for hundreds of miles inland, while the coast-line is studded with large cities, like Melbourne, Sydney, and Adelaide, and with numerous flourishing settlements. On the other side is the enormous tract of Western Australia, 1300 miles in length from north to south, and 800 miles in breadth, thus embracing in extent one-third of the continent.

Here, instead of ports, of towns, and of settled districts, we find only a few scattered settlements, and this is the case though the colony is an old one, and one for which much has been done. By virtue of seniority of settlement, it ranks next to New South Wales. It was founded in 1829, under Government auspices, and with a great flourish of trumpets, mainly in consequence of a very favourable report prepared by Captain Stirling, R.N., afterwards Sir James Stirling, first Governor of the colony. To induce settlement, enormous grants of land were made to men of influence and capital, who in return were to bring out a proportionate number of labourers, and perform other 'location duties.' Thus a Mr. Peel, a relative of Sir Robert Peel, obtained 250,000, Colonel Latour 103,000, and Sir James Stirling 100,000 acres.

It appears now to be agreed that this grant system was as injudicious as it was lavish. Middle-class capitalists came to reside on their estates, and not to work, and the settler of humbler but more useful pretensions was led to believe that the colony was closed to him. The settlement was hapless from the first. Old colonists give lively descriptions of how ladies, blood horses, pianos, and carriages, were landed on a desolate coast, while no one knew where his particular allotment lay. The settlers found that they had no control whatever over the men they brought out, and in some instances they were left to establish their homes in the wilderness as they best could by themselves. Many, deciding from the arid appearance of the place that there was no prospect of success, abandoned it. Some who believed at one time that the Garden of Eden lay on the banks of the Swan River, and that colonisation was a perpetual picnic, returned wiser, poorer, and sadder, to the more congenial sphere of settled and civilised England. Others, like the Messrs. Henty, sought more favourable fields, and ultimately, in *Australia Felix*, acquired both riches and reputation. Many of those who remained do not seem to have possessed the stuff the real settler is made of, but thought more of giving entertainments and seeking pleasure than of work. When the supplies they had brought from England ran out, they were very nearly starved, and they had to expend much of their capital in importing provisions.

In after years their numbers were but little increased. Considerable doubt existed about their progress being sure, and none whatever about its being slow. Never well-to-do, they felt very severely the depression general throughout Australia in 1848. People looked to their money-chests only to see if they had sufficient left to take them away. Casting about for relief, the York Agricultural Society suggested that convicts should be applied for, and the proposal found favour with the people. Backsliding seems as easy with communities as with individuals. The colonists who had met more than their share of difficulties and obstruction, while proceeding in the straightforward path of settlement, found everything prepared for them when they turned aside. It so happened that, just before this time, the effects produced by the vast influx of convicts into Tasmania had shocked the British public, and provoked a spirit of resentment and resistance in the Australian colonies such as had never existed before. The whole of the eastern settlements stood arrayed against the mother country, and the conclusion was forced upon the Imperial Government that the system must be terminated. Earl Grey, who was then in office, and who had initiated important improvements in the management of convicts, endeavoured to find for the flood of British criminals a new outlet where these plans could be tested. He addressed a circular on the subject to the colonies of New South Wales, South Australia, Western Australia, New Zealand, the Cape, the Mauritius, and Ceylon, explaining the improvements it was proposed to make in the management of the convicts, promising to send a free emigrant for every convict shipped, and asking whether, under these conditions, the colonies would consent to receive criminals. The answer was "No" in each instance, with the single exception of Western Australia. Her reply was favourable, and a bargain was soon struck. Western Australia entered into the contract upon the understanding that the annual imperial expenditure should be sufficiently large to be of importance to the colony, and in the hope that cheap labour would attract capital to it.

The system was continued until 1868, when, in deference to the protests of the sister states, and because also expectation had been greatly disappointed as to the results, convict importation was finally closed and determined. The protest was carried so far that it was proposed by one Government to exclude from the ports of the free colonies ships that had come from the convict settlement; and this decision would have shut out the mail steamers. And Western Australia found that, while it obtained convict labour, it frightened away free men, while immigrants avoided the place as though it were a plague-spot. Now it may be said the past is forgotten, the taint is dying away, and Western Australia is awakening into life.

The country is being opened to the northward, but up to within the past few years the bulk of the settlement was in the south-western corner of the colony, in the neighbourhood of the Swan River—a stream which possesses the peculiarities of being short, broad, and shallow, and which, in consequence of its bar and its flats, is well-nigh useless as far as navigation is concerned. At the mouth of the river lies Fremantle, with a population of about 5000 —the seaport of the colony. Ten miles higher up is Perth, the capital city, possessing 2000 more inhabitants than Fremantle. A like distance farther on is pretty Guildford, and seventy miles from the seaboard, separated from it by the Darling ranges, are the agricultural settlements in the Avon valley. The town of Bunbury lies on the western sea-coast; and Albany, a settlement of equal size on the southern coast, is indebted for its existence to its harbour—King George's Sound—being a place of call for the mail and numerous other steamers. Geraldton and Roebourne are northern ports —the latter the centre of the pearl fishery trade.

Looking at its vast size, and the dispersion of its thin population—the whole not equal to that of a Melbourne suburb—Western Australia can only be described by one image—it is the giant skeleton of a colony.

A clever Yankee once described the colony of Western Australia as having been run through an hour-glass. The American, however, possessed the failing common to many humorists: he economised the truth for the sake of uttering a smart saying. It is only to be expected that in a country like Western Australia, possessing an area of a million square miles, that sandy tracts are to be met with; but to assert that the colony is a vast sandy waste—a Sahara—is to convey a wrong impression of its physical features. In the far north the richest of Australian tropical vegetation exists; fine rivers flow through tracts of splendidly grassed territory, and the conformation of the country is bold. It is farther south, where the tropical growth gives place to level plains and bush vegetation, that the dreary sandy plains exist in parts, though not to the extent sometimes imagined.

Along the south-west coast, however, where the splendid forests of jarrah and other varieties of eucalypts are found, the soil is richer and better watered, but the prevalence of dangerous poison plants renders it less useful for pastoral purposes. Some districts are infested with strong quick-growing bushes, the juices of which are fatal to animal life. There are no less than fourteen known varieties of these plants, but only four are commonly pointed out. These are the York-road, the heart-leaf, the rock, and the box-scrub—the *Gastrolobium bilobum*, the *Gastrolobium calycinum*, *Gastrolobium callistachys*, and the *Gastrolobium anylobiaides*. The most common is the York-road plant, a low bushy scrub, with narrow fresh green leaves, and a light coloured stem. After a bush fire this plant is the first to spring up. Its young shoots have a particularly green and attractive appearance; the sheep feed eagerly upon it, swell to a great size, and die in a few hours. A single mouthful at this period is sufficient to destroy them. The plant is also very dangerous when in blossom, as then also the sap is fresh and plentiful. In summer, when it is dried up, the sheep do not care about it, and may even be fed on country where it is not very thick. It is destructive to horned cattle, but it does not affect horses much. Millions of acres are overrun with this poison shrub, which, however, when cleared, may be profitably occupied. For instance, in the mahogany forests about the Darling ranges, there is a coarse grass growing which would support sheep well, but, in consequence of the prevalence of poison, at present the land remains unproductive and unoccupied. As one goes north the poison plants disappear, and the flocks which Victoria and Queensland and New South Wales are now pouring into the new pastures there feed as securely as they would in the Western District of Victoria, or on the famous Darling Downs.

The city of Perth is built in a picturesque situation above the broad reach of the Swan River known as Perth Waters. Its streets are broad and well defined, and, considering that it only contains a population of some seven thousand souls, it is a remarkably compact town. The Town Hall, built by convict labour, is a pretentious structure, and within easy distance of it are to be found the Legislative Assembly Chamber and the commodious offices devoted to the use of the civil servants. The principal buildings are to be found in St. George's Terrace, a fine wide street lined with beautiful trees. The soil of Perth is admirably suited to the growth of many varieties of fruits and flowers, and the love of the residents for these gifts of nature

GOVERNMENT HOUSE, PERTH.

is indicated by the well-kept gardens that surround most of the houses. Indeed, no colony can produce finer fruit than Western Australia.

Fremantle, the principal port of the colony, is a modest little town with narrow streets nestling at the mouth of the Swan River. Here was maintained for many years the great convict depôt of the colony, and the many public conveniences the residents possess are due to the efforts of prison labour. The most remarkable feature about Fremantle is the whiteness of its streets and buildings. This arises from the almost universal employment of limestone as a building and road material. The glare on a bright summer's day is both extremely dazzling and hurtful to the eyesight. The Swan, which runs from Fremantle to Perth, is a noble river. It opens out into splendid reaches of varying width. Its banks are fringed with veteran gum-trees, whose rugged outlines are reflected with mirror-like sharpness in the clear waters beneath. The misfortune is that such a fine stream cannot be made practical use of without considerable expenditure; but all entrance to it from the sea is barred by a ridge of sandstone, which stretches, some six feet under water, completely across its mouth.

The southern portion of the colony is singularly unfortunate in possessing very few harbours. Fremantle is now an open roadstead, but the State proposes by the expenditure of a large sum of money to give effect to a scheme formulated by Sir John Goode, the eminent engineer, which, it is believed, will render the port perfectly safe in all weathers. King George's Sound, however, has been exceptionally favoured by nature. The entrance to it is by either of the two passages which surround the massive rock, appropriately named Breaksea, that rises up with rugged abruptness in the centre of the channel. At the rear of Breaksea the inlet opens into a grand harbour, where the largest ships can lie with perfect safety in the roughest weather. The scenery along the shores is diversified and beautiful, and no more charming place of call could be found for the ocean mail steamers, which anchor there regularly every fortnight. The little town of Albany is situated upon the rising boulders of granite at the head of the sound; but its isolated position has told against the prosperity of the place. The harbour has been aptly stated to be the front gate of the colony, with a blank wall behind it. That blank wall consists of the long tract of dismal country lying between Albany and Perth; but the colonists hope, with the aid of an English syndicate who have contracted to construct a railway to join the Government system at Beverley, to abolish the barrier which now cuts them off from Albany. They will then be able to utilise the harbour and to elevate it to the position it should occupy. Of late years the strategical importance of King George's Sound in case of warfare has commanded the attention of Imperial and Colonial statesmen.

The climate of Western Australia is decidedly salubrious. For years past the residents have sought to induce the Indian authorities to make it their sanatorium for invalid officers, but so far nothing definite has resulted from their representations. Sport is plentiful in every part of the province, and the homely hospitable character of the people renders a visit to the colony a most enjoyable experience. The great pride of Western Australians is in the wild flowers that cover their plains in the spring time. The surface of the earth is then carpeted with an endless variety of the most beautiful forms of the floral creation. Every crevice and cranny is filled with blossoms, whose bright colours contrast vividly with the more delicate hues of the 'everlastings' that abound in the more level country.

The pearl fisheries off the coast of West Australia, and expecially at Shark Bay, produce the true pearl oyster, the *Avicula margaratifera*. For a long time this shell was supposed to be valueless, on account of its thin and fragile structure; but now there is a great demand for it, both in Europe and America. It is especially prized by French and German artists for fine inlaid cabinet work. During the year 1883, 619 tons of pearl shell were exported from Western Australia, valued at $4000, and the value of the pearls exported during the same period was $20,500. Several of these pearls were of extraordinary size and beauty, one weighing 234 grains. A mass of pearls in the form of a perfect cross was found at Nickol Bay, West Australia, in the early part of last year, each pearl being about the size of a large pea, and perfect in form and colour.

The oysters in the West Australian fisheries are generally removed by passing an iron-wire dredge over the banks, but divers are also employed, the diving being carried on from the end of September to the end of March. Pearl oysters are gregarious in their habits, and whenever one is met with it is almost certain that vast numbers of others will be found in the immediate neighbourhood.

ALBANY.

Writing of Western Australia, Sir F. Napier Broome, C.M.G., says: 'Many of the farmsteads I visited in the country districts are such as their owners may well be proud of. They represent years of arduous toil, and of courageous struggle with many difficulties. I find in some of them the grey-haired, sturdy early settlers of the colony, still strong and hale, after nearly a half-century of colonisation, now able, I was rejoiced to see, to rest from their labours, and to enjoy growing comforts and easier circumstances, while the farm or the sheep station was looked to by the stalwart sons. Wherever I went, I perceived that Western Australia, though not a country of richness, was nevertheless a land in which an honest worker of shrewd wit has rarely failed to gather round him, as years went on, the possessions which constitute a modest competence, and perhaps something more, enjoyed amidst the affections and the ties of a home in which he can take life easily in the evening of his days, and from which he can see his children marry and go forth to such other homes of their own. I did not find the feverish, brand-new, shifting and disjointed communities of a wealthy colony, but I found a people amongst whom ties of kindred are numerous and much thought of, who have dwelt side by side with each other all their lives, and who have preserved among themselves a unity and friendly feeling most pleasant to encounter, and social characteristics natural and agreeable in their unaffected-ness, simplicity and heartiness. Each little township resembles an English village rather than the colonial assortment of stray atoms one is familiar with elsewhere. The more one sees and knows of Western Australia and its people, the more they win on one.'

The most important circumstance in connection with the Western Australia of to-day is the discovery that the north-western corner contains fine pasture-land, permanent rivers, and good harbours. Explorers from the east have visited the place, and have reported favourably upon its prospects, and now there is a good deal of *bonâ fide* squatting enterprise being displayed. Companies have been formed, and syndicates and flocks and herds have been sent from Melbourne and Sydney by sea, and cattle are also being pushed across from Queensland. If these ventures have only half the success which is predicted for them, there is a great future in store for this part of Western Australia. And recent reports from the colony disclose the fact that there is every indication that an extensive gold-field exists in the country between King Sound and Cambridge Gulf. A 'rush' has set in, and there is considerable excitement throughout Australia about the matter.

TASMANIA.

VIEW OF MOUNT WELLINGTON, TASMANIA.

CORRA LYNN, TASMANIA.

CHAPTER IX.

TASMANIA.

A HOLIDAY RESORT FOR AUSTRALIANS—LAUNCESTON—THE NORTH AND SOUTH ESK—MOUNT BISCHOFF—
A WILD DISTRICT—THE OLD MAIN ROAD—HOBART—THE DERWENT—PORT ARTHUR—CONVICTS—FACTS
AND FIGURES.

THIS island is the smallest of the Australian colonies, and the lover of the picturesque pronounces it to be the fairest of them all. It is a land of mountain and of flood—another Scotland, but with a perennial blue sky and an Italian climate. Now that there is a leisured and a wealthy class in Australia, this wealth of scenery is becoming a real fortune to Tasmania. A twenty hours' run takes the holiday-maker from Melbourne wharves to Launceston, and then the island, with its streams, its hills and its fisheries, is open to him. The rush of excursionists to enjoy the cool weather and the romantic views has become greater and greater with successive years; and, though New Zealand is the Switzerland of the colonies, yet Tasmania, being so much nearer the mainland, and having so many native charms, is sure to hold its own as a holiday resort.

Moreover Tasmania is held in affectionate regard by thousands of Australians whose birthplace she is. Her material prosperity is not so great as that of her neighbours, and consequently her youth are lured to the mainland, where they usually establish themselves successfully, and where they also acquire such substance as enables them at frequent intervals to revisit the old land. So great is the migration of the young men that it would have fared ill with the damsels of the isle but for a compensatory influence. Their own youth were lured away to seek for wealth and to woo wives in other lands; but the Tasmanian clime enriches the fair sex with complexions which are the despair of their more sallow sisters of the north, and the deserted maidens have always had their revenge by captivating and winning their visitors. His lady friends tremble for the Australian bachelor who spends a leisure month across the straits. And then there are many territorial families in Victoria and New South Wales whose sires emigrated from Tasmania in the early days of colonisation. It is not surprising therefore that there is a strong attachment between the rich sons and the poorer motherland which it will take much to sever.

Bass Straits separate Tasmania from Australia, but the journey is easily made in large well-equipped steamers which leave Melbourne regularly, and which speedily reach the smooth water of the Tamar. This river debouches on the north coast, and is a noble stream forty miles in length, coursing through alluvial stretches backed in the far distance by grand tiers of mountain ranges. Along its banks there are dots of settlement, but, as they are at wide intervals, the traveller appreciates the charm of navigating what appears to be an unexplored tract. But for the beacons and buoys to mark the shoals there is little to indicate the presence of man. Given a clear day—and all days are more or less clear in Tasmania—a bracing breeze from the south, and a trip up the Tamar cannot be excelled; and if it be that the traveller comes in the early spring, before the snow has quite disappeared from the highest hills beyond, and while the freshness of the new vegetation still makes the near landscape glorious, he will wish for no better communion with nature.

Launceston, on the Tamar, is the second city of the island—second in point of picturesque surroundings, second also in political importance, because Hobart, in the south, is the capital; but first in the material aspect, from which point of view even lovers of the beautiful are content to pay some homage. It is decidedly a pretty town. At its wharves two rivers, the North Esk and South Esk, meet, and in their mingling form the Tamar. The North Esk comes down over crags and precipices, through a striking gorge, whose bold sheer cliffs frown at each other and on the deep silent stream below. The most romantic spot of all is Corra Linn, on the South Esk, where the river dashes over boulders through a gateway of basalt, changes into a quiet restful stream, reflecting foliage and rock in its peaceful depths, and then dashes on again, falling and falling and falling, cataract after cataract, whirlpool after whirlpool, until its force is expended in the deep Tamar, and its bosom becomes dotted with the 'white-winged messengers' of commerce. The South Esk flows through rich agricultural

ON THE SOUTH ESK, TASMANIA.

country, where the land has been farmed for more than a generation, and where the hedged fields on the hillsides recall Kent and Sussex to the mind of the Englishman, and give the average Australian, whose knowledge of farm landscape is made unpleasant by the recollection of mile after mile of rail fencing, a splendid idea of how husbandry may be made to present a charming aspect.

A fine railway runs through fertile country to the town of Deloraine, on the River Menader, and on to the north-west coast to the mouth of the Mersey, a distance of eighty miles. It passes large properties devoted to the breeding of high-class sheep, which have served to make the colony famous throughout Australia, because the flocks which now supply a vast proportion of the world's wool have been bred from studs imported from these areas.

The train passes through glades and over plains, round mountain sides and over streams; and at Deloraine the traveller is delighted by the bold appearance of Quamby Bluff, jutting from the end of a long range against the blue sky. The Mersey has beauties, and so have the Don, the Cam, the Forth, and numberless other limpid streams which 'bring down music from the mountains to the sea'—this music being particularly grateful to the visitor who, it may be, has just left the parched plains of Central Australia.

Back from this coast, through wild country to wilder, lies Mount Bischoff, the richest tin mine in the world. This prize was secured, unhappily not for himself, by an old gentleman voted eccentric by his neighbours, but so strongly inspired with the belief that rich tin deposits must exist in the interior that for months and months he would wander through the bush prospecting under conditions of hardship scarcely conceivable—a long way from the tracks of humanity, absolutely self-reliant and thoroughly confident. At last, where a pretty river, the Waratah, turns a prominent hill and runs over a high precipice, he found the long sought-for treasure. He also found on his return to the haunts of men that his story was not believed, that 'Philosopher Smith,' as he was designated, was not able to easily secure the assistance requisite for the development of his discovery. In time, however, he succeeded, and the Mount Bischoff Company was formed, and started upon its career. Mr. Smith held his allotment of stock through the early years of work, but gradually he was compelled to realise in the market at ridiculously low rates. Twelve years ago the shares went almost begging at thirty shillings each, and they have since ruled as high as eighty pounds. It is difficult, on looking at the mine, to conjecture when the lode will be exhausted. The 'faces' being worked from part of the mountain, and as the material is brought under treatment, of course, the picturesqueness of the scene has to suffer.

When 'Philosopher Smith' broke upon it he must, if he was anything of a philosopher, have been greatly impressed with its magnificence, for then not only were the mountains lofty, but they bore magnificent forests, and the babbling streams were delightfully pure. Now the traveller can only admire the mountains, which are still high, unless, of course, he is also impressed by the enterprise which has drawn the wealth from the hillside, albeit that in so doing the forests have suffered and the waters have been stained.

Beyond Mount Bischoff the woods grow denser, and traffic through them to newer tin-fields on the west coast is infrequent and hazardous. Twelve or fifteen years ago very few men visited that district, and even now nobody goes there unless impelled by strong business reasons. When you stand on Mount Bischoff and look across the hills which rise in this wild region, you are presented with a grand spectacle, and you wonder if the day can ever come when clearings and cultivation will be where now the bush appears to be impenetrable.

From Launceston, in an easterly direction, the traveller finds much to interest him, particularly in that quarter where stand Ben Lomond and other

VIEWS IN TASMANIA.

mountains, each upwards of 5000 feet high. St. Mary's Pass is a natural gateway through the ranges, and the coaches which traverse the road rattle along alarming ridges; but pleasure and surprise are so strongly excited that there is no time for a thought of danger. Through to Fingal, and on to St. Helen's at George's Bay, on the east coast, the variations of scene are endless. And then the cliffs are reached; and, gazing on the broad blue ocean once more, it is vividly brought home to the continental Australian that he is on an island, and a beautiful island also. Tin and gold mines have been worked in this division of the colony more or less successfully; but the interests were not permanent, and the attention of investors has long since been diverted to finer fields.

Launceston is connected with Hobart by one of the finest macadamised roads—120 miles in length—in the world, and by a narrow-gauge railway of 132 miles. The railway is a comparatively new institution, but the road has stood for years, and will stand for ages. In 'the old days,' as the past is happily and conveniently termed in Tasmania, there were only two settlements—Hobart and Launceston; and it became as necessary to establish

LAUNCESTON.

others as to connect them. At that time hundreds of convicts were being landed from England, and the additional necessity to find employment for them induced the governing authorities to embark upon the enterprise of making the road and making new towns. It cost more than a railway would cost nowadays, for prison labour has always been expensive. But it is thoroughly substantial, and has the great advantages of passing through the richest agricultural and pastoral lands of the colony, and the great charm of running over many bold hills and of crossing many of the most beautiful streams of the island. Thirteen hours were required to perform the journey

HELL GATE, TASMANIA.

between the two towns when coaches were running, and there are many who, while thoroughly appreciating the quicker transit of the railway, nevertheless sigh for the good old invigorating coach-ride, and the rests at the old hostelries—just such as would be found on an English turnpike. The railway had to be constructed along a devious course, and consequently traffic was diverted from the direct road, and from the ancient hamlets to newer settlements, where everything is spick and span. The old resting-places have not yet disappeared, but many of them are decaying, and present striking contrasts to the new order of things on the rail route. 'For a young country you have an elegant supply of ruins,' was the comment of an American who was driven over this road. He was quite right, but the ruins are revered by all who remember the traffic when it was at its best. They are not signs of national decay, but the result of a change of transit.

As they stand now even they are not unprofitable. Without them many a picturesque scene would be less interesting.

Hobart is a lovely city. It has been made beautiful by nature, and it will become famous by the act of man, for it is the spot where the first Federal Council of Australasia met in January 1886. It is rather inverting the order of things to first dwell upon the newest characteristic of the town, but the departure is justified by the promise of the great good which must follow the establishment of the Union. In due course the federal spirit must expand, and when Australians, in years to come, revert to the starting-point of their national life, they will think kindly of Hobart.

The city of 'balmy summers and cheerful winters' stands on the big-volumed Derwent. The river rises far inland, up among high mountains, where Lake St. Clair and Lake Sorell reflect the snowy peaks of their basaltic guardians. It runs through rich country, where settlement has become permanent, down to New Norfolk, where it bends and twists, and skirts lofty cliffs, passes through hop-fields, whose golden crops in the autumn make the landscape beautiful and the air fragrant, develops into a noble course a little farther on, and at Hobart is in some places seven miles in width, and in no place less than a mile. There are high mountains on both sides, and the valleys are exceptionally productive. The city is seated on seven hills; behind it is Knocklofty, a respectable eminence; and behind that again Mount Wellington, 4166 feet in height, forms a grand background. The population numbers about thirty thousand, and the citizens are tolerably thrifty, although not so enterprising nor so wealthy as the colonists of the mainland. The city was established early in the century, and for very many years it was the *entrepôt* for the thousands of wretched convicts expatriated from Great Britain. It was an important military station, and its palmiest days were thirty-five years ago, when the Imperial Government spent £1000 a day in the maintenance of the gaols and the barracks. At that time the city was an important place, but the curse of transportation was upon it. In 1851 the last convict ship discharged its cargo, and since then the system has gradually run down, and is now very little more than a memory. The traces must necessarily linger, but their ultimate effacement is only a question of time. It is a pity that so fair a spot was ever used for so ill a purpose.

Being the capital, Hobart possesses all the usual official institutions: a Government House in a beautiful garden on the Derwent, in which resides a well-paid representative of Her Majesty; Parliament Houses, in which sit two Chambers, who legislate upon the most approved constitutional plan; a Supreme Court, Civil Service Court, and other accessories suited to the requirements of the colony. Its monetary and trading institutions are sound, and its commercial relations with other ports expanding. The harbour is lined with well-built wharves, and the depth of water is astonishing. Twelve miles down the river are the Heads. The Southern Pacific is beyond; and so easy is the navigation that vessels very rarely have to employ pilots. Reefs and shoals are unknown.

A two or three hours' trip seawards to the south-east enables one to reach the famed Port Arthur, in a land-locked bay hedged by bluff promontories whose aspect is so stern that the beneficent calm within is made the more beautiful when they are passed. Port Arthur was the centre of convictism for many years, and the prisons stand now, though the place has long since been given up as a penal settlement. It is on the southern point of a peninsula, which is connected with the mainland by a narrow strip, not more than one hundred yards wide, called Eaglebank Neck. This was, and is, the only means of communication by land with the outer world, and the authorities devised stringent if inhuman means to prevent the escape of prisoners. Fierce dogs were chained at such intervals that it would be impossible for a man to pass between them, and they kept watch by night, while armed men were on guard by day. It was a straight and narrow path, but no one ever passed that way. To swim through the water on either side was equally hazardous, because of the risk of being attacked by sharks, and consequently the number of escapes was extremely small. The only authenticated break away from bondage was performed by three men—Martin Cash, Cavanagh, and Jones, who swam Pirates' Bay in the night, reached a farm-house before morning, equipped themselves for highwaymen's work, and defied arrest for some years. The last prisoners were removed from Port Arthur in 1876, and the magnificent buildings, than which there are none better in the world, have been allowed to decay, the rich fields and meadows, which were pictures in the busy days of the establishment, are fast becoming obliterated, and desolation promises to encompass all. Slowly but surely Nature is reclaiming her own, and is effacing the memorials of an infamy which none care to look back upon. Chapter after chapter might be written upon the annals of Port Arthur, but they would be inconsonant with the tone attempted to be given to these pages.

On the west of the mouth of the Derwent is a magnificent channel forty-five miles in length, deep and beautiful. It is called D'Entrecasteaux Channel, after an early French navigator, and is a passage-way to Hobart for ships coming from the westward. It is lined with fine harbours, and among other rivers receives the Heron, which comes down through dense forests from the region referred to in the remarks made concerning the view from Mount Bischoff. This is indeed a wild country, but hardy adventurers have made homes among the giant trees and slowly cleared patches for fruit-gardens and farms. Far back on the west coast is Macquarie Harbour, which was a convict station before Port Arthur, and whose history is willingly being forgotten.

Tasmania contains an area of 26,300 square miles, so that she is a little smaller than Scotland, and a little larger than Greece. Her population on

January 1st, 1885, was 130,541. Her total revenue was £549,000. She had 215 miles of railway open, and she was constructing 160 miles. Her exports were valued at £1,475,000, and her imports at £1,656,000. All English fruits—such as the strawberry, the raspberry, and the apple—grow with a marvellous profusion, and the hop industry flourishes.

ON THE RIVER DERWENT.

SECTION III.

AUSTRALIAN LIFE AND PRODUCTS.

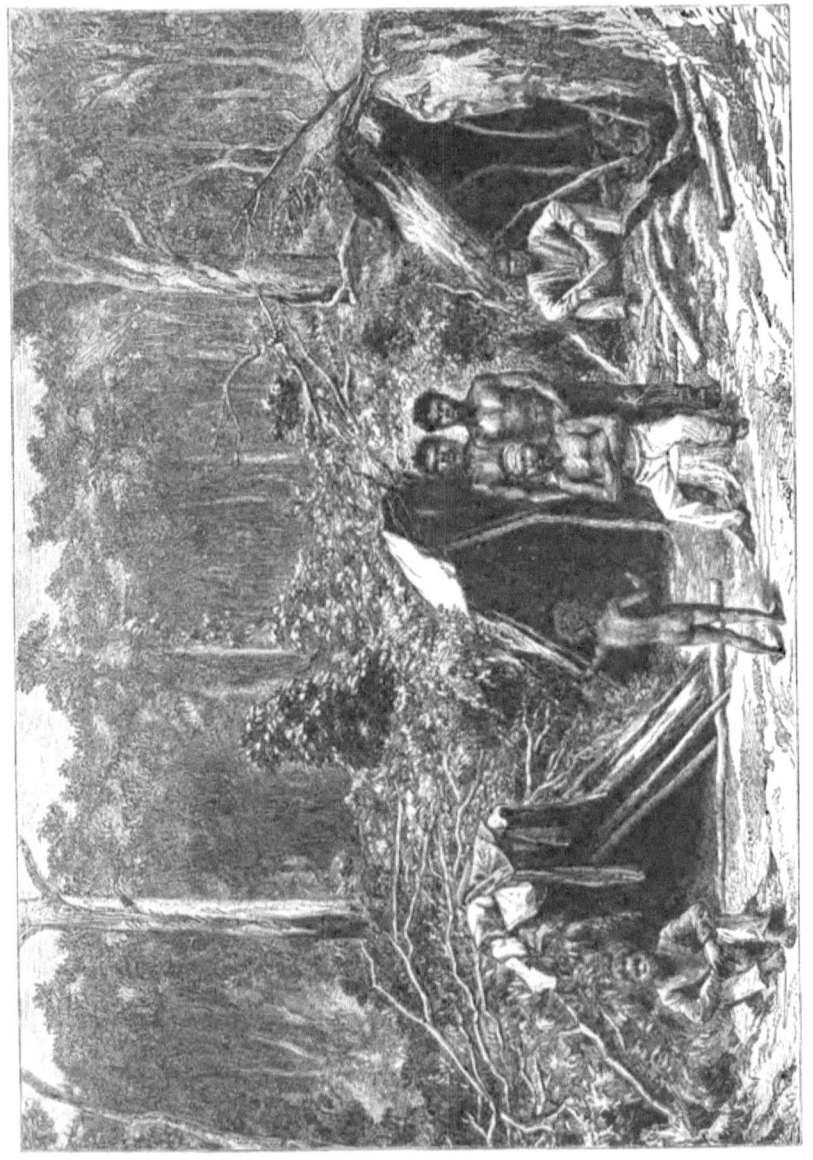

Native Encampment.

A NEW CLEARING.

CHAPTER X.

HEROES OF EXPLORATION.

TRAGIC STORIES—FLINDERS AND BASS—ADVENTURES IN A SMALL BOAT—DISCOVERIES—DISAPPEARANCE OF BASS—DEATH OF FLINDERS—EYRE'S JOURNEY—LUDWIG LEICHARDT—DISAPPEARANCE OF HIS PARTY—THEORY OF HIS FATE—THE KENNEDY CATASTROPHE—THE BURKE AND WILLS EXPEDITION—ACROSS THE CONTINENT—THE DESERTED DEPÔT—SLOW DEATH BY STARVATION—LATER EXPEDITIONS.

THE story of Australian exploration is for the most part of a tragic character. Great geographical results have been achieved, but the price has been paid in great sacrifices. The records of success are saddened by many episodes of disaster and of death.

The tale of heroism and suffering begins with Bass and Flinders, two young men who have left their names writ large upon the map for ever. They went out in 1795 with the second Governor of New South Wales, Bass as surgeon of the ship Reliance, and Flinders as midshipman. The two were soon friends; they had an equal love of adventure, and the new circumstances in which they were placed fired their ardent imagination with the hope of discoveries that should benefit mankind, if not bring reputation to themselves. Never did enthusiasts set to work with more scanty material. With a little boat eight feet long, and a boy to help, they cleared Sydney Heads, and faced the unknown Southern Ocean, and mapped out a section of the Australian coast. They used to row or sail as far as they could in the day, and at night throw out a stone, which served them as an anchor, and lie at these primitive moorings till daylight. Many were their narrow escapes by sea and shore.

Once they were upset near the shore; their powder was wet, and they lost their supply of fresh water. On reaching land and righting the boat, a body of natives came down upon them, and, as the savages were well armed and were hostile in their demeanour, it looked as if the defenceless party would be sacrificed. But after a hurried consultation Bass spread the powder out on the rocks to dry, and went off to a creek to fill the keg with fresh water, while Flinders, trading on the personal vanity of the blacks, and their love for hair-dressing, trimmed the beards of the chiefs with a pair of pocket-scissors. He had no lack of candidates. Long before he had finished his task, Bass had repacked the dry powder, had loaded the muskets, and the two friends with a rush regained their boat, leaving many would-be customers lamenting, and disappointing probably some would-be slayers. A few weeks afterwards a vessel called the Sydney Cove was wrecked in the unsurveyed Tasman seas, the escaping boats were thrown ashore in a storm near Cape Howe, and this very tribe massacred most of the crew.

Ingenuity and boldness rescued the adventurers from one peril after another. As their exploits attracted attention, their friend Governor Hunter helped the discoverers to some small extent. Flinders had to sail with his vessel to Norfolk Island, but Bass obtained a whaleboat and a crew of six men, and with this aid he pushed boldly along the coast of what is now the colony of Victoria, discovered Corner Inlet and Western Port, and proved that Tasmania was an island, and not, as was then supposed, a part of the mainland. The separating strait rightly bears his name to this day.

On the return of Flinders, Governor Hunter placed a small sloop, the Norfolk, at the service of the friends, and with it they surveyed the entire coast of Tasmania, Flinders preparing the charts. Their discoveries were numerous, the river Tamar being among them. This, alas, was the last joint expedition of the gallant comrades! Bass was tempted to join in some trading speculation to South America, and unhappily his vessel was confiscated by the Spaniards for a breach of the customs laws. Bass was sent as a prisoner to work in the silver mines, and was never heard of more. Well can it be imagined that many a hope, many a bright career, many a noble aspiration, have perished in those living tombs, but surely they never closed over a bolder or more unhappy victim than Bass.

Flinders for a time continued his successful career. He visited England, and was raised to the rank of lieutenant, and he was authorised to proceed with his surveys in a vessel called the Investigator. A passport was obtained for him from the French Government, exempting him from capture during the time of war. At the same time, however, the French Government sent out an expedition under M. Baudin. With characteristic energy, Flinders did his work in advance of his French rival, who was driven by scurvy to Sydney. Flinders was returning home when the state of his rotten vessel forced him to put into the Mauritius, which then belonged to France. Here, despite his passport, his ship was seized, and he was thrown into prison. M. Baudin called at the Mauritius soon afterwards, and he is

SPLITTERS IN THE FOREST.

accused by history of a great treachery. Certainly there is much that charity finds it difficult to explain in M. Baudin's conduct. It is written that he copied the charts and papers of the prisoner. This seems to be an incredible meanness; but it is certain that he connived at the detention, and that on his return to France he published a work anticipating all that Flinders could say, ignoring the labours of the prisoner, and representing himself as the great Australian discoverer of the day.

More than six years elapsed before Flinders was released; and, upon reaching England, he found that the discoveries he intended to announce had been given to the world, and that the public was familiar with them. Exposure, hardships, and, above all, the long weary years in the French prison, had all told upon him. He set to work to bring out his book and his charts, and just managed to complete his task, but sank immediately afterwards. It is a mournful chapter. But the fame of Flinders survives and is growing. In Australian annals no name is more justly honoured.

Very soon the colonists began to push inland from their settlements on the coast, feeling their way, and gradually becoming acquainted with the novel features of their new abode. There was great joy when, after many endeavours, a Sydney party discovered a pass through the extraordinary precipices of the Blue Mountains, which had long hemmed in the infant colony. The adventures of Oxley, who thought that he was stopped by an inland sea, of Sturt, who nearly perished in the Central Desert, and of Mitchell, who opened up the Western District of Victoria, have already been incidentally mentioned in these pages.

One of the first efforts to reach the centre of the continent was made by Edward John Eyre, in after-days Governor of Jamaica. He left Adelaide in 1840, his party consisting of five Europeans and three natives, with thirteen horses. But the year was one of drought. The great marsh, now called Lake Torrens, was a sheet of glittering salt. The horses broke through the crust, and a hideous and tenacious black mud oozed out. Advance on this line was impossible; and, upon taking a more westerly route, the explorer was stopped by the still larger marsh now called Lake Eyre, which was also a deceptive sheet of salt. Disappointed, Eyre returned to the head of Spencer's Gulf, and decided to make a dash at Western Australia, following the line of the cliffs in order to intercept any rivers. Alas, there were none to intercept! The party had to depend for subsistence upon the chance of finding water-holes not dried up, and the little clay pans formed by the aborigines, and called native wells.

At an early stage Eyre sent all his party back, except his overseer Baxter, his black boy Wylie, and two natives. The farther he went the more sterile the country became, and the worse was his position. The burning sand suffocated the travellers, and day after day passed without water. Most of the horses died. Eyre was watching the remnant feeding on some scanty vegetation one night, and was musing on his gloomy prospects, when he heard a musket shot. The two natives had murdered the overseer, decamped with the stores, and left Eyre and his boy Wylie to their fate! The night was dark, and Eyre gives a vivid description of his feelings as he sat in the gloom by the side of the corpse of his friend, expecting every moment that the treacherous blacks would use their muskets upon him and Wylie. He could not bury the body, for the ground was hard rock, and he had no tools. Day after day he plodded on. Had Wylie deserted him he must have perished, for in the boy's quickness in detecting traces of the natives and indications of their 'wells' lay the only chance of safety. At last, when nearly exhausted, Eyre saw two boats at sea. They belonged to a French whaler. Eyre was taken on board, was well fed, was supplied with stores and ammunition; and, after a rest of eleven days, he and Wylie continued their journey, and, the country improving, they reached King George's Sound in safety.

Thirty years after this journey was made it was repeated from the opposite side by Mr. John Forrest, a fine young West Australian explorer, who with a small party passed over it with but little inconvenience or difficulty. Mr. Forrest again and again camped on Eyre's old camping ground, which he recognised at once, and which seemed to have remained undisturbed from the time Eyre and Wylie left it.

Next comes the tale of the explorer over whose fate a veil of mystery and romance has fallen. In 1844 Ludwig Leichardt was an eager young German botanist. He set his heart upon exploration. His first trip was most successful, as, starting from Sydney, he made his way to the Gulf of Carpentaria, and discovered many of the fine rivers of Northern Queensland. So much enthusiasm was occasioned by these revelations of a grand country in tropical Australia that the Sydney people subscribed £1500 for Leichardt, and the Government presented him with £1000. After a short trip of seven months in the Queensland bush, Leichardt organised an expedition to cross Australia from west to east, a feat which no man has yet performed, though explorers from the west have met the tracks of those coming from the east. His party consisted of H. Classen, six white men, and two blacks, with cattle and sheep. His last letter, which was dated from McPherson's Station, Cogoon, April 3rd, 1848, concluded in the following words: 'Seeing how much I have been favoured in my present progress, I am full of hopes that our Almighty Protector will allow me to bring my darling scheme to a successful termination.'

The hope was not realised. He has been tracked to the banks of the Flinders, in Northern Australia, but his fate is unknown. The disappearance of his party has been absolute, and the Australian imagination has dwelt long, anxiously and lovingly upon the mystery. No theory has been so wild but that it has found some eager adherents; every straw of hope has been grasped at. Expedition after expedition has sallied forth to rescue the living or to bury the dead, but all in vain: the tales have proved false, and slowly hope has faded away.

The explanation now generally accepted is that the party was surprised in low country by some tropical flood, in which all perished. A capital bushman, Leichardt was not likely to starve. And if he had died from thirst, or if he had been murdered by the natives, some of his animals would probably have escaped, or some weapon or some piece of their equipment would have been found, and would have furnished a clue to the mystery. But the earth gives no more trace of him than the deep sea of a vessel that has foundered, or the air of a bird that has passed by.

The Kennedy disaster was on a large scale. Edmund Kennedy had

AFTER STRAY CATTLE.

explored the course of the Barcoo with success, and in 1838 he was landed with twelve men at Rockingham Bay, to strike across country, to a schooner at Cape York. The dense jungle of the tropical bush and the vast swamps checked their progress. He left eight men at Weymouth Bay, and proceeded with three men and a black boy, Jacky, on his journey to the schooner. The blacks were numerous and hostile, and the bush gave them shelter. Kennedy was speared by an unseen hand, and died in the arms of Jacky. The three men were never heard of, and only two of the other party of eight escaped. Jacky, however, turned up at the schooner with the papers confided to his care, a living skeleton. He is one of the many instances of the fidelity of the Australian black when once he has become attached to his master.

The rush to the gold-fields checked exploration for a time. All thoughts were directed to the auriferous treasure. But after the new population had settled down somewhat, a strong desire manifested itself to discover the secret of the continent. The South Australian Government offered a reward of two thousand pounds to the first person who should cross the continent from south to north, and the intrepid John McDouall Stuart was soon in the field to earn the money and to secure the fame. Stuart had been one of the officers in Sturt's last party, and he had discovered for South Australian employers a fine belt of pastoral territory beyond the salt lakes that had discomfited Eyre. In Victoria the public subscribed a large sum of money, which the Government doubled. The Government also sent for camels, at a great expense, and the Royal Society appointed a committee to organise the expedition. The command was given to Robert O'Hara Burke; Landells, who had brought over the camels, was second; and a young man from the Melbourne Observatory, W. J. Wills, was placed in charge of the instruments. The dash and energy of O'Hara Burke, and the talent and Christian fortitude shown by Wills, have endeared the memory of both these leaders to the country; but the admission must be reluctantly made that the tragic issue was due to Burke's unfitness for the command. He was no bushman, and was too eager and impulsive for a leader. As a second in command he would have been invaluable; as a chief he was overweighted.

The expedition left Melbourne August 20, 1860. Burke's orders were to take his stores up to Cooper's Creek, and, when he had established his depôt there, to start for Carpentaria. On the way up Burke quarrelled with Landells, who resigned, Wills taking his place. At the same time Burke met with a man named Wright, who struck his fancy, and this stranger, utterly unqualified for the post, was placed in an important command. Burke left the bulk of the stores and most of the party on the Darling in charge of Wright, who was to bring them on with all possible speed, while the leader made a forced march with a light party to Cooper's Creek. Days passed without Wright's appearing; and, instead of returning to hasten up his stores, Burke, with characteristic boldness, resolved to make a dash for Carpentaria. He divided his party and his stores, leaving Brahe and three men at the creek to wait for Wright, and started with Wills, King and Gray, on December 16, with six camels and a horse.

The party made a rapid journey through fair and good country. Box forests and well-grassed plains—a good squatting country—was traversed, and finally the explorers struck a fine stream, the Concherry, running to the north, whose banks were clothed with palms and tropical vegetation. They were greatly pleased, for they knew they had but to follow this river to reach the northern sea. But the camels broke down. Leaving them in charge of Gray and King, the leaders proceeded on foot, and came with exultation to an inlet of the great Northern Gulf.

Their task was done; they could turn back. But this was their last moment of joy, troubles thickening afterwards to the end. Their rapid travelling over broken country under a tropical sun, with scanty rations, began to tell upon all. There was no time for rest nor for hunting. The party must push on and on to reach the depôt where food awaited them. Gray complained of a failure of all his powers, and in particular of an inability to use his legs. It was thought he was shamming, and he was punished and hurried on; but soon afterwards he laid down and died, and the same symptoms attacked them all, Burke bitterly regretting his severity. They began to kill their camels, and, scarcely sustained by this food, they pushed on, their pace dwindling to a crawl, and then to a totter. On April 21 they came in sight of the depôt, and a grateful 'Thank God!' burst from their lips. They fired a gun. It was not answered, and they found the place deserted. Wright, with the stores, had never reached the creek, and Brahe, seeing week after week elapse, had fallen back to ascertain what was the matter in his rear, leaving half of his remaining provisions for Burke and Wills.

When the three travellers entered the desolate depôt they gazed round in dismay, and Burke threw himself on the ground to conceal his feelings—they had expected safety, and they were confronted by death. But a tree marked 'Dig' caught their eyes, and they came upon the buried provisions. A rest for a couple of days was indispensable. And then Burke came to the decision not to strike for the Darling, as Wills desired, but to make for a pioneer cattle station at Mount Hopeless on the South Australian border. This was a fatal choice, the camp being a few miles away. The same day Brahe, who had met Wright, rode back to the depôt. By one of those fatalities which mark the expedition, Burke had buried his despatches in the *cache*, and had taken some pains to restore it to its original condition, and so Brahe thought it had not been disturbed. It was clear that some disaster had happened to Burke. But Wright, who was in command of the stores, decided to fall back on the Darling to report matters to the committee. Thus were Burke and Wills abandoned. Wright and Brahe, when at the depôt, were within two hours' journey of the perishing leaders. Growing weaker and weaker, the forlorn and deserted trio struggled on. The country became worse and worse. They struck the wretched desert where Sturt suffered so severely. Water failed there, and all vegetation disappeared, and all hope of food, from the country. Their torn and rotten clothing dropped from their backs. They killed their last camel. In despair they walked back to Cooper's Creek, on the chance of finding the natives—just at the moment when another day would have rewarded them with the sight of Mount Hopeless on the horizon.

When they regained the creek their provisions were gone. The blacks

MONUMENT TO BURKE AND WILLS IN MELBOURNE.

showed the hapless men how to gather the little black seeds of a grass called the nardoo, on which they mostly lived themselves. The white men hoped that it would support them, but could only starve upon it. An effort was made to reach the depôt to see if relief had arrived, but the strength of Burke and of Wills gave out. Wills was the first to sink. As he could travel no farther, Burke and King left him in a native hut with nardoo seed and water by his side, while they sought assistance from the blacks, who had given Wills a meal of fish a few days before. When King returned a few days later with three crows which he had shot, the pure and gentle spirit of Wills had taken its flight. Burke had only tottered a few miles from the hut. He laid down to die, asking King to place his pistol in his hand, and not to bury him. The strong man had become as a child. He sent many messages to friends. Then he was silent; and the early morn saw the earthly end of a generous, ardent, manly leader, whose faults were of the head and are forgotten, while his virtues were of the heart and endear his memory.

King made his way to the natives, with whom he lived many months, until he was rescued. The Government granted him a substantial pension. A married sister devoted herself to his care. But those who looked upon his face saw his fate there. Thirst, hunger, and privation had smitten him too severely, and very soon he also fell asleep.

Great energy was shown in sending expeditions to the relief of Burke and Wills, when Wright returned to the Darling without them. One party under M'Kinlay started from Adelaide, another under Walker from Queensland; Landsborough led a third, which was landed at the Gulf of Carpentaria to reach Melbourne, and Howitt proceeded from Melbourne *viâ* Cooper's Creek. The knowledge these expeditions gave of the country was great, and when McDouall Stuart, in 1862, crossed the continent, interest in exploration lapsed. Ten years afterwards a series of efforts were made by Giles, Gosse, Lewis, Forrest and Colonel Warburton, to cross from South Australia to the western seaboard. Forrest pushed his way through from the west, and Warburton from the east. This latter party had a terrible battle for life, and without the camels, and without an intelligent black fellow who hunted for the native clay-pans, all must have perished. The men abandoned everything, even their clothing, down to shirts and trousers; and Warburton arrived, strapped to a camel's back, rapidly sinking from exhaustion.

Still there are vast territories in Australia untrodden by the foot of the white man, but the task of filling up the blanks is now left to the pioneer settler. One squatter pushes out beyond another, as the coral insect builds on its predecessor's cell. Without any stir a district that was once in the desert is occupied, and then the blocks beyond are attached. The process is sure, though without sensation.

A GLANCE AT THE ABORIGINES.

A CORROBOREE.

A WADDY FIGHT. (See p. 168.)

CHAPTER XI.

A GLANCE AT THE ABORIGINES.

FIRST ENCOUNTER WITH THE BLACKS—MISUNDERSTANDINGS—NARRATIVE OF A PIONEER—CLIMBING TREES—THE BLACKS' DEFENCE—DECAY OF THE RACE—WEAPONS—THE NORTHERN TRIBES—A NORTHERN ENCAMPMENT—CORROBOREE—BLACK TRACKERS—BURIAL—MISSION STATIONS.

FROM large portions of the continent the native has now been absolutely swept away. The immigrant who intends to settle in the populated parts of South Australia, Victoria, New South Wales, Tasmania and Queensland, will have no more to do with the natives than he would have to do with the Redskins if he visited Ohio or Pennsylvania. The aborigines, unless in the harmless guise of mission blacks, are not to be found except in the far-off outlying parts where the pioneer squatter is prosecuting his labours, and there the old sad tale of plunder and of murder by the tribes, and of revenge by the white man—too often on guilty and innocent alike—is still repeated.

The blacks of Australia differ in appearance and in size greatly, quite as much as do the inhabitants of Europe. There are poorly fed tribes who are correctly described by Dampier, while on the other hand men of a splendid physique can be found amongst them It may be said at once that the tales that deny their intelligence and which degrade them almost to the level of brutes are unfounded. They live in their natural state, without care or responsibility, very much as children, and they have the cleverness and the uncertain tempers and the mercurial happiness of children. They could live, it must be remembered, with a minimum of exertion. So long as a country was not over-populated, opossums, fish and roots were obtained with little labour, and there was no occasion for house-building. As animals like the sheep and the horse flourish in the open in most parts of Australia without artificial shelter, so man can 'camp out' with comparative ease. Thus the black was not, and is not, called upon to exercise his higher faculties. Food was too scarce to enable him to multiply and to form permanent settlements. Yet, such as it was, its collection did not brace him up to any mighty efforts. His life was never in danger from wild animals. If he found many opossums, he indulged in a surfeit; if marsupials, lizards, birds and roots were scarce, he pinched for a time. If the black had discovered agriculture, his state might have been very different, but of cultivation he never had the slightest idea. Once when a tribe was induced by an enthusiastic settler to plant potatoes, the men and women rose in the night and dug up the seed and feasted upon it. It was inconceivable to them why the white man should desire to bury good food.

Thus the black man wandered in one sense aimlessly over vast tracts of country, living on its chance fruits: a restless nomad, with no apparent prospect of rising on the social scale. Even in Victoria, the garden of Australia, it took 18,000 acres to maintain a black. It must be admitted that this waste of power was too great. The European had a right to conceive that the land was not in an occupation that need be respected, though more consideration for the original tenants might have been and ought to have been shown. The mischief was that colonisation was unsystematic. No one knew how to deal with the blacks. The blacks did not know how to establish friendly relations with the white man.

We give two illustrations here of Victorian natives. The likeness in profile is that of a civilised black, and is strongly characteristic of the Victorian race. The woman is also a good representative of the Victorian lubra. In civilised races the woman eclipses the man in beauty, but the rule reads backwards in savage races. The Australian black man is often stately and picturesque—his mate is generally hideous.

An offence committed within a tribe was generally settled by the disputants fighting the issue out with spears or with waddies until the elders thought that justice was satisfied. Terrible wounds would be given and received, but to the healthy black man, cuts, smashes, and bruises that would be fatal to the white are as nothing.

Although many pioneer settlers lived on friendly terms with the blacks, yet their sheep would be stolen, and then there were reprisals. Here and there all the hands on a station would be sacrificed. When the settlers were at all near each other, it was the custom in Victoria to fix heavy bells on posts near the house, and thus the warning of an attack was passed through a district, and a force would be brought together to relieve the white men and to punish the black. So it has been in turn in all the settlements.

Mr. G. F. Moore, when Advocate-General at the Swan, gave the following narrative of a defence made to him by a black, who for his crimes had been outlawed: 'A number of armed native men had surrounded the house, when Mr. Moore went to the door to speak to them, having his firearms close at hand. He soon recognised Yagan, but the natives near the door denied that he was present. However, when the outlaw perceived that he was known, he stepped boldly and confidently up, and, resting his arm on Mr. Moore's shoulder, looked him earnestly in the face, and addressed him, as the first law officer of the Crown, to the following effect: "Why

CIVILISED ABORIGINES.

do you white people come in ships to our country and shoot down poor black fellows who do not understand you? You listen to me! The wild black fellows do not understand your laws; every living animal that roams the country and every edible root that grows in the ground are common property. A black man claims nothing as his own but his cloak, his weapons, and his name. Children are under no restraint from infancy upwards; a little baby boy, as soon as he is old enough, beats his mother, and she always lets him. When he can carry a spear, he throws it at any living thing that crosses his path; and when he becomes a man his chief employment is hunting. He does not understand that animals or plants can belong to one person more than another. Sometimes a party of natives come down from the hills, tired and hungry, and fall in with strange animals you call sheep; of course, away flies the spear, and presently they have a feast! Then you white men come and shoot the poor black fellows!" Then, with his eagle eye flashing, and holding up one of his fingers before Mr. Moore's face, he shouted out—"For every black man you white fellows shoot, I will kill a white man!" And so with "the poor hungry women: they have always been accustomed to dig up every edible root, and when they come across a potato garden, of course, down goes the wanna (yam-stick), and up comes the potato, which is at once put into the bag. Then you white men shoot at poor black fellows. I will take life for life!" And so far as in him lay Yagan kept his word.'

Generally speaking, the colour of the natives is a chocolate brown; their dress is of the simplest kind: the opossum cloak, the strips of skin worn round the loins and the apron of emu feathers constitute their wardrobe. The aboriginal is essentially a hunter. His hands reveal his occupation at once, as they exclude the idea of manual labour. An English ploughman, it has been said, might squeeze two of his fingers in the hole of an Australian shield, but he could do no more. Like most nomads, the objection of the natives to steady work is insuperable. In pursuit of game, in stalking an emu or a kangaroo, they will concentrate their attention for hours, and will occasionally undergo great fatigue, but without some excitement or object they will do nothing. No black man will ever stoop to lift an article if he can raise it with his toe. And the big toe of the black man in the bush is almost as useful and as flexible as the thumb. The missionaries at the blacks' stations have achieved wonders with their pupils, but the one thing they cannot do is to induce the pure aboriginal to labour in any such way as the white man works. Give him a horse, however, and he is happy.

Mr. E. M. Carr, Chief Inspector of Stock in Victoria, in his interesting and valuable *Recollections of Squatting in Victoria*, brings the daily life and the customs of the blacks vividly before the reader. His father took up country so far back as 1839, in the Moira district; and Mr. Carr, though a stripling, was left in charge. He came in contact with the blacks therefore when they were absolutely in a state of nature. He gives a long and interesting account of some matrimonial negotiations carried on between the Ngooraialum and Bangerang tribes. We have space for only a small part of his graphic story. The young people are betrothed to each other years before the time of marriage, and, of course, have no voice whatever in the arrangements. While Mr. Carr was staying with the Ngooraialum tribe, the Bangerang, preceded by one of their number named Wong, arrived. 'The Bangerang, after they had satisfied themselves by a glance that it was really Wong, continued as if entirely unconcerned at his arrival; taking care, however, to keep their eyes averted from the direction in which he was coming. This little peculiarity, I may notice, is very characteristic of the blacks, who never allow themselves to give way to any undue curiosity as regards their fellow-countrymen, and as a rule refrain from staring at any one.

Wong, when he arrived within twenty or thirty yards of the camp, slowly put his bag off his shoulder without saying a word, gazed around him for a moment in every direction save that of the Bangerang camp, and sat down with his side face towards his friends, and quietly stuck his spears one by one into the ground beside him, with the air of a man who was unconscious of any one being within fifty miles of him ; the Bangerang, in the meantime, smothering all signs of impatience. Probably five minutes passed in this way, when an old lubra, on being directed in an undertone by her husband, took some fire and a few sticks, and, approaching the messenger, laid them close before him, and walked slowly away without addressing him. Old Wong, as if the matter hardly interested him, very quietly arranged his little fire, and, as the wood was dry, with one or two breaths blew it into a blaze. Not long after, an old fellow got up in the camp, and, with his eyes fixed on the distance, walked up majestically to the new-comer and took his seat before his fire. Though these men had known each other from childhood, they sat face to face with averted eyes, their conversation for some time being constrained and distant, confined entirely to monosyllables. At length, however, they warmed up ; other men from the camp gradually joined them ; the ice was broken, and complete cordiality ensued ; and Wong having given the message of which he was the bearer, that the long-expected Ngooraialum were coming, the conference broke up, the new-comer being at liberty to take his seat at any camp-fire, at which there was no women, which might suit his fancy. The next evening, from amongst the branches of a tree in which they were playing, some young urchins announced the arrival of the Ngooraialum. The bachelors, being unencumbered, arrived first ; next, perhaps, couples without children ; then the old and decrepit ; and, lastly, the families in which there was a large proportion of the juvenile element. As they arrived they formed their camps, each family having a fire of its own, some half-dozen yards from its neighbour's ; that of the bachelors, perhaps, being rather further off, and somewhat isolated from the rest. After the strangers had arranged their camps (which, as the weather was fine, consisted merely of a shelter of boughs to keep off the sun), and each group had kindled for itself the indispensable little fire, which the aboriginal always keeps up even in the warmest weather, they began to stroll about. On this occasion two or three Bangerang girls found husbands amongst the Ngooraialum, who returned the compliment by making as many Bangerang men happy. In every instance it was noticeable that the husband was considerably older than the wife, there being generally twenty years—often much more— between them ; indeed, as I frequently noticed, few men under thirty years of age had lubras, whilst the men from forty to fifty had frequently two, and occasionally three better halves.'

In another chapter Mr. Carr shows his friends in an unamiable light.

One of the warriors of the tribe died. 'Pepper' was buried with all honours; but, as usual, the great question was who had bewitched him. The common practice was resorted to for discovering the enemies.

'Shortly after sunrise the men, spear in hand (for no one ever left the camp without at least one spear), went over to the new grave. Entering its enclosure, they scanned with eager eyes the tracks which worms and other insects had left on the recently-disturbed surface. There was a good deal of discussion, as, in the eyes of the blacks, these tracks were believed to be marks left by the wizard whose incantations had killed the man, and who was supposed to have flown through the air during the night to visit the grave of his victim. The only difficulty was to assign any particular direction to the tracks, as in fact they wandered to and from every point of the compass. At length one young man, pointing with his spear to some marks which took a north-westerly direction, exclaimed, in an excited manner: "Look here! Who are they who live in that direction? Who are they but our enemies, who so often have waylaid, murdered, and bewitched Bangerang men? Let us go and kill them." As Pepper's death was held to be an act particularly atrocious, this outburst jumped with the popular idea of the tribe, and was welcomed with a simultaneous yell of approval which was heard at the camp, whence the shrill voices of the women re-echoed the cry.

'A war-party, fifteen in number, proceeded stealthily, and chiefly by night marches, to the neighbourhood of Thule station, visiting on their way those spots (known to one of the volunteers) at which parties of the doomed tribe were likely to be found. After several days' wandering from place to place, subsisting on a few roots hurriedly dug up, and suffering considerably from hunger and fatigue, they caught sight, as they were skulking about towards sundown, of a small encampment, without being themselves seen, upon which they retired and hid in a clump of reeds. About two o'clock in the morning the war-party left their hiding-place and returned to the neighbourhood of the camp, and having divested themselves of every shred of clothing, and painted their faces with pipe-clay, they clutched their spears and clubs, and, walking slowly and noiselessly on, soon found themselves standing over their sleeping victims.

'According to native custom, no one was on watch at the camp, and I have often heard the blacks say that their half-starved dogs seldom give the alarm in cases of strange blacks, though they would bark if the intruders were white men. They gently raised the rugs a little from the chests of the doomed wretches, and at a given signal, with a simultaneous yell, plunged their long barbed spears into the bosoms or backs of the sleepers. Then from the mia-mias, which were quickly overturned, came the shrieks of the dying, the screams of the women and children, blows of clubs, the vociferation of the prostrate, who were trying to defend themselves; the barking of the dogs and the yells of the assailants, who numbered fully three to one.

Altogether it was a ghastly, horrible scene that the pale moon looked down on that night at Thule.'

Mr. Carr describes the agility displayed by the men in such feats as mounting the trees for opossums, &c., and the illustration on page 12 tells the story of one of these hunts.

Of Australian weapons the most interesting is the boomerang. Mr. Brough Smyth, in his work on the aborigines, discredits the idea that there is any connection between the boomerang and the throwing or crooked stick of the Dravidian races of India, as has been contended, and insists that it is *sui generis*. Its peculiar action depends upon a twist in the wood, the twist of the screw, which may be imperceptible to the careless observer, but which is always there.

When a skilful thrower takes hold of a boomerang with the intention of throwing it, he examines it carefully (even if it be his own weapon, and if it be a strange weapon still more carefully), and, holding it in his hand, almost as a reaper would hold a sickle, he moves about slowly, examining all objects in the distance, heedfully noticing the direction of the wind, as indicated by the moving of the leaves of the trees and the waving of the grass, and not until he has got into the right position does he shake the weapon loosely, so as to feel that the muscles of his wrist are under command. More than once, as he lightly grasps the weapon, he makes the effort to throw it. At the last moment,

A BOOMERANG.

when he feels that he can strike the wind at the right angle, all his force is thrown into the effort : the missile leaves his hand in a direction nearly perpendicular to the surface ; but the right impulse has been given, and it quickly turns its flat surface towards the earth, gyrates on its axis, makes a wide sweep, and returns with a fluttering motion to his feet. This he repeats time after time, and with ease and certainty. When well thrown, the farthest point of the curve described is usually distant one hundred or one hundred and fifty yards from the thrower. It can be thrown so as to hit an object behind the thrower, but this cannot be done with certainty. The slightest change in the direction of the wind affects the flight of the missile to some extent ; but the native is quick in observing any possible causes of interference.

The northern blacks are the southern blacks, but are 'much more so.' They are finer and fiercer men ; more given to slaughter, building better houses, more intractable. The engraving on the next page depicts an encampment of blacks on the shore, at the mouth of Wreck Creek, Rockingham Bay, Queensland. The figure to the right of the picture is engaged painting a shield. The curiously shaped huts of the North Australian blacks form characteristic objects in the engraving.

The engraving on page 166 of a corroboree in the far north is from a photograph by Mr. P. Foelsche, at Port Essington. The males group themselves as shown in our illustration, and stamp the ground with both feet simultaneously, making a peculiar sound, and keeping tune with a guttural exclamation. The first who sounds a false note or misses a beat leaves the group amidst the ridicule of the bystanders, and this process is continued until the number of performers is reduced to a pair, who divide the honours. These northern tribes are guilty of revolting acts of cannibalism.

A NATIVE ENCAMPMENT IN QUEENSLAND.

No keener observers of nature in the world are to be found than the Australian blacks. Their gaze is microscopic rather than extensive. They have no appreciation of natural beauty and taste; but their attention is directed to the broken twig, the crushed grass, the displaced stone, the light impression—to anything and everything that may reveal the proximity of a foe or the presence of food. No such trackers exist anywhere. Celebrity has recently been thrust upon them. In 1880 a gang of marauders took to the bush in Victoria. They committed many daring crimes, and the police were unable to check or to capture them, though the best men in the force were employed, and tens of thousands of pounds were spent.

The idea of employing black trackers was mooted, and some of the

Victorian aborigines were first tried. But civilisation dulls the instinct. Trackers were obtained from the far north, who did their work well. The criminals were surprised and brought to bay. Three were killed in the conflict, and the leader, who was captured severely wounded, was hanged in Melbourne Gaol. It was acknowledged on all hands that the presence of the trackers paralysed the gang, and a few blacks have been kept about Melbourne ever since.

So soon as the black has been dispossessed, and has ceased to be dangerous, the heart of the white man relents towards him, and he proceeds to look

A NATIVE TRACKER.

after the remnants of the tribes. Philanthropists, lay and clerical, find liberal support from the state and from individuals. Thus Government stations and mission stations are called into existence in Victoria, in South Australia, in New South Wales, and in Western Australia, where the blacks have homes provided for them and food, and where strenuous efforts are made to improve their morals and to Christianise them. They are taught to grow hops and to look after cattle and to repair their fences, but it is all essential that reserves and streams should be at hand in which they can hunt and wander. Under these favourable circumstances the full-blooded black is dying out ; and, as there is a movement to distribute all half-castes amongst the general population, the time will come when these institutions will be closed, owing to a lack of inmates. The visitor should not miss the opportunity of inspecting one of the establishments, most of which are easily reached. Illustrations are given here of the Lake Tyers station, which is under the charge of the Rev. J. Bulmer. A railway journey of a

CHURCH, SCHOOLHOUSE, AND ENCAMPMENT AT LAKE TYERS.

hundred miles to the town named Sale, and steamer thence to the entrance of the Gippsland lakes, brings the visitor to the spot, and he is sure of a hospitable reception. The upper view represents the mission church, a handsome building, constructed of wood, and erected by the Rev. Mr. Bulmer. Service is held morning and evening. Other sketches show the school building, in which the aboriginal children are taught by Mr. Morriss, state school teacher; and a native camp, occupied by natives who decline the accommodation of the huts.

There are many missions to the blacks. How far is the race capable of Christianity? On such an issue only one who has closely studied the natives can pronounce an opinion. If there is any one person who is more entitled to be heard on the subject than another, it is the Rev. F. A. Hagenauer, who has had nearly a thirty years' experience with the Australian black. Mr. Hagenauer came to Australia in 1858 as a Moravian missionary to the aborigines, and has been engaged in his self-denying labours ever since. Recently he has associated with the Presbyterian Church of Victoria, and he has acted—without any stipend from the state—as manager of the Government aboriginal station, Ramahyuck. The following letter speaks for itself:—

ABORIGINAL MISSION STATION, RAMAHYUCK, GIPPSLAND,
January 30, 1886.

DEAR SIR,—I gladly comply with your desire, to furnish you with some reliable information as to my views and experiences among the aborigines in reference to their capability of understanding and receiving Christianity as a power to change the hearts and lives of these people.

The beneficial influence of true Christianity, through the progress of education and civilisation, has worked a wonderful change in the lives, manners and customs of the blacks. Any one not acquainted with their former cruel and most abominable habits, but knowing them only as now settled in peaceable communities, would scarcely believe that the description of heathen life which the apostle Paul gives in the Epistle to the Romans was a correct picture of their mode of life. Given to the continual licentiousness of their carnal minds, they were slaves to their lusts and passions, which, working with their superstitious and cruel nature, made them ever ready, and their feet swift, to shed blood. Without a settled home, they wandered about from place to place in a most miserable and depraved condition, adding to their native vices drunkenness and other evils, which they had learned from white people. The different tribes, either from superstitions or family quarrels, or from violation of tribal territory and the sacred surroundings of their dead, were at continual warfare; and their fear of revenge by secret enemies was sometimes terrible to behold. Their howling noises for many days and weeks before and after the deaths of their friends and relatives, which told but too plainly that they were without hope in this world, were most pitiful to hear, and the disgusting scenes in connection with their nocturnal corroborees cannot be fully described. Added to this came the tormenting custom to which some of them were subjected at their peculiar native festivities, and especially the barbarous treatment of females by their tribal lords. It is not necessary to refer to the many atrocities and crimes committed by them in days gone by, for it is well known that they gave trouble to the earlier settlers, and were a terror to lonely women and children in the bush; nor need I say anything about their loathsome diseases, which were prevalent among them in consequence of their immoral lives and habits. Having lived for so many years among them as a close observer, I can testify that the above statements give only a faint picture of what actually took place, for there is not one hour of the night or day in which I did not witness one or other of their cruel customs.

In the midst of their quarrels and bloody fights, at their ghastly corroborees, and during the time of their most pitiful cries around their sick and dead ones, we have been able to bring to them the Gospel of life and peace, and many times did they throw down their weapons and stop their nocturnal dances in order to listen to the Word of God and the joyful news of salvation through our Lord Jesus Christ. In the beginning of 1860 a remarkable awakening amongst the blacks began with earnest cries to God for mercy, and sincere tears of repentance, which was followed by a striking change in their lives, manners and habits. The wonderful regenerating power of the Gospel among the lowest of mankind worked like leaven in their hearts, and, through patient labour and the constraining love of Jesus, we were soon privileged to see a small Christian church arise and a civilised community settled around us. To the glory of God it can be said that a comparatively large number of the remnant of this rapidly decreasing race has been brought to the knowledge of the truth, and a good many honoured the Lord by their humble Christian life for many years, and a still greater number died in full assurance of eternal happiness through faith in Jesus Christ.

The old manners and customs of the blacks have changed even among the remaining heathen under the influence of the Word of God. The war-paints and weapons for fights are seen no more, the awful heathen corroborees have ceased, the females are treated with kindness, and the lamentable cries, accompanied with bodily injuries, when death occurred, have given place to Christian sorrow and quiet tears for their departed friends. With very few exceptions, all the wanderers have settled down as Christian communities on the various stations, and, where they are kept under careful guidance and religious instruction, the change from former days is really a most remarkable one.

Whilst, on the one hand, we have reason to rejoice that God has blessed His work to such an extent, we feel sorrow at stating that our joy is often mingled with disappointment, in so far that so very many of these people pass away either through the consequences of their former diseases, or for some unknown reason. The Lord does what seemeth good in His sight; and we have reason to thank Him for so many tokens of His grace, and for the triumphs of the Gospel in the redemption of those members who passed away in peace to their eternal home, to be for ever with the Lord.

The carrying out of the Saviour's commandment to His Church, to preach the Gospel to every creature, has accomplished that which was considered by many an impossibility; for the influence of the Word of God proved its Divine power, and many of these poor depraved blacks soon began to sit at the feet of Jesus, 'clothed, and in their right mind.' General civilisation and education, in and out of school, for young and old, followed step by step as a fruit of true Christianity, and showed in reality a greater progress than we ourselves could have expected in accordance with the generally adopted opinion in reference to the capability of the aborigines.

I may state here that in every case of conversion we have been most careful and cautious not to administer the ordinance of baptism too soon, but only after long trials and careful instruction in the Word of God. Some of the converts have honoured their confession of faith by most honest, faithful, and consistent lives from beginning to end; some have been, and still are, weak in their Christian course, whilst others have often to be reminded, and have even had to be put under Christian discipline, in consequence of backslidings and sins; but even of those it can be stated truthfully that, though weak, they did cling to Jesus for salvation, and cried for mercy to Him who alone can forgive sins.

To enter into particulars of individual conversions and triumphs of faith would be out of place in such a short statement as this; but there are very many instances, both of young people, and of the very oldest aborigines, who lived and died as faithful humble Christians. On the whole, I believe that there is not any great difference between these blacks and any new converts from the heathen in other lands, or even among some classes of white people. It may also be stated that many people here and elsewhere at once expect the converted aborigines to be model Christians, whilst they forget that Christianity truly teaches all to grow in grace and in truth, and with patience and perseverance to press forward to the great aim; and this certainly is carried out by the converted aborigines in this colony.

I remain, dear sir, yours very truly,

F. A. HAGENAUER.

SOME SPECIMENS OF
AUSTRALIAN FAUNA AND FLORA.

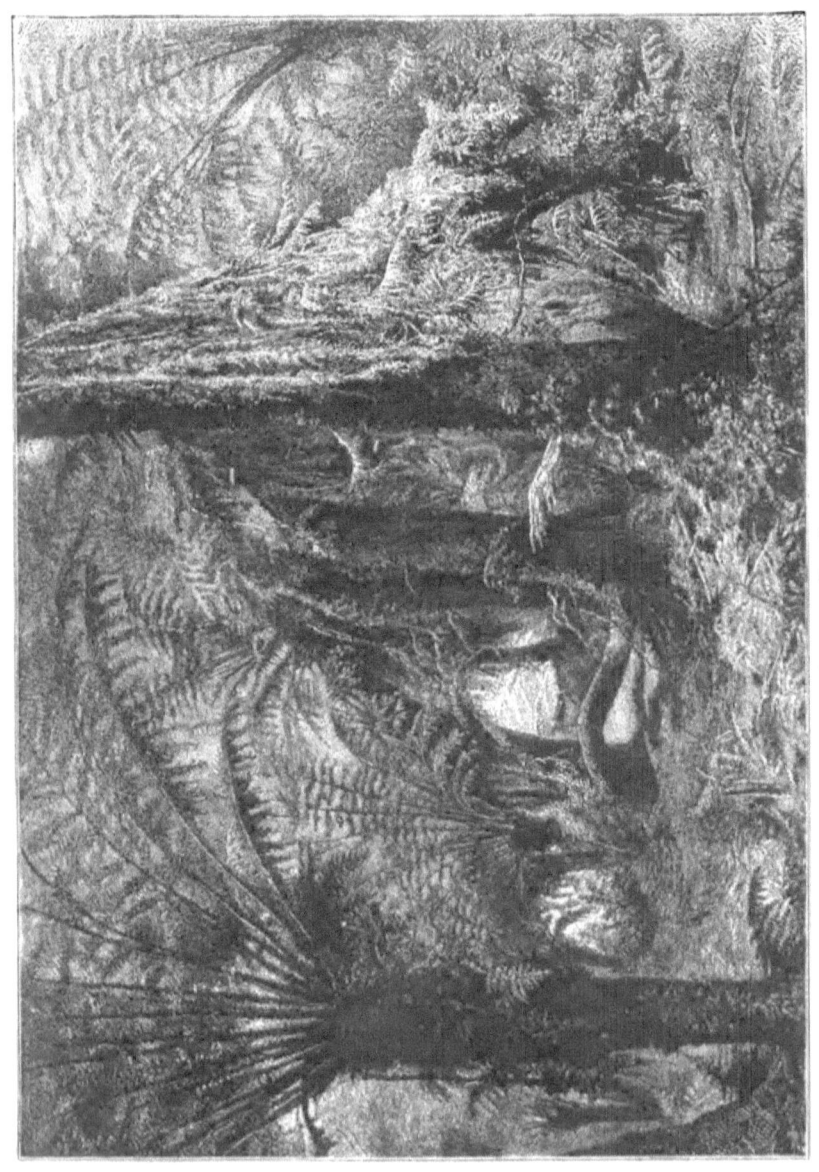

Australian Tree-Ferns.

DINGOES.

CHAPTER XII.

SOME SPECIMENS OF AUSTRALIAN FAUNA AND FLORA.

MARSUPIALS—THE 'TASMANIAN DEVIL'—DINGOES—KANGAROO HUNTING—THE LYRE-BIRD—BOWER-BIRD—THE GIANT KINGFISHER—EMU HUNTING—SNAKES—THE SHARK—ALLEGED MONOTONY OF VEGETATION—TROPICAL VEGETATION OF COAST—THE GIANT GUM—THE ROSTRATA—THE MALLEE SCRUB—FLOWERS AND SHRUBS.

NO large carnivorous animals roam over the Australian plains, to endanger the life of man or to destroy his flocks and herds. Australia is the mother country of the meek and mild marsupial, which is found in abundance, varying in size from the great red 'old man' kangaroo, which stands between six and seven feet high, to the marsupial mouse, which will sleep in a good sized pill-box. There is the stupid, heavy wombat, which seems a mere animated ball of flesh, which burrows in the ground, and which apparently cannot move a mile an hour when it appears on the surface, though its pace is really better than that. On the other hand, there is the elegant flying fox, or rather flying opossum, which by means of a bat-like membrane glides through the air at night, astonishing the traveller, who sees hundreds of large forms sweep noiselessly by. Great fruit-eaters are these flying foxes, and there is tribulation when a horde visits a settled district. The native bear, as a marsupial sloth is termed, is the most innocent-looking of animals, and the most harmless, feeding on the leaves of the gum. It swarms in the various colonies. In the next tree will be found a family of the *Dasyuridæ* or native cats, beautiful spotted creatures, the size of a half-grown cat, whose sharp face and continuous activity betray at once a restless and a wicked disposition. It is carnivorous, fierce and intractable. The marsupial pictured on page 183 is a specimen of an elegant variety of the common opossum, found principally in the neighbourhood of the Bass River, Victoria. The common opossum is found everywhere.

While the native cat is the only mischievous carnivorous marsupial on the Australian mainland, Tasmania is possessed of two much larger and more destructive animals, the *Thylacinus* or 'tiger-wolf,' and the *Sarcophilus* or 'Tasmanian devil;' the former is nearly as large as a wolf, and is shapely and handsomely marked with stripes on the flanks. The

THE *Sarcophilus* OR 'TASMANIAN DEVIL.'

latter is a smaller animal. It has been described as 'an ugly bear-like cat.' It is a thick-set creature, black in colour, with white patches, and its hideous appearance and its untameable ferocity quite entitle it to its popular designation. Both 'tiger' and 'devil' are nocturnal, and both have been so hunted and trapped by the settlers, whose sheep and poultry they killed, as now to be very scarce. Neither has ever been known to attack man. At one time, as geological examination shows, the marsupial 'devil' and his relative were both found in Australia, and the wonder is that they should have so completely disappeared from the scene as they have done.

An animal that stands entirely apart from the marsupials in Australia is the wild dog. The dingo is one of the mysteries. Whence did he come? He is allied to the wild dogs of India, but why should this Indian animal be in Australia—his form on the surface and his bones in ancient deposits— while no other representative of the fauna of the Old World is known? Leaving science to unravel this problem, it may be said of the dingo that he is a good-looking but an ill-behaved animal. He is compared to the sheep-dog, to the wolf, and to the fox, and, in fact, he has a dash of each of these creatures in his appearance. He is about two feet high, is well-proportioned, with erect ears and a bushy tail. He stands firmly on his legs, and shows a good deal of strength in his well-constructed body. His colour varies from a yellowish-tawny to a reddish-brown, growing lighter towards the belly; and the tip of his brush is generally white. He cannot bark like other dogs, but he can howl, and he does howl with a soul-chilling effect. His note is to be likened unto

BASS RIVER OPOSSUM.

The wolf's long howl from Oonalastra's shore.

Campbell's melodious line conveys the idea of misery, and discomfort and uneasiness are engendered when the slumbers of the sleeper in the bush are disturbed by the blood-curdling cry of these breakers of the nocturnal peace. The blacks used to catch the puppies of the wild dog, and then train them to hunt, but they found the European dog sufficient for their purposes, and much more docile and affectionate. As dingoes worry sheep, the first task of a squatter is to get rid of them. When they breed in shelter and a semi-settled district—if they can issue from mallee scrub—a handsome reward is always offered for their heads. In parts of Victoria as much as £2 per head is paid. An engraving of the creature is given on page 181.

Man has to be fed, and therefore game has to be shot and fish has to be caught. The animal life of Australia had little rest when the blacks roamed over the country, but it has still less, now that the white man is in possession. The kangaroo hunt varies from a necessary slaughter of the blue and red kangaroos of the plains, to an exciting run and desperate fight for life at the finish of it, when the game is the big dark forester living in the timber belts that line most of the Australian streams. The battue of

A KANGAROO BATTUE.

kangaroos is often rendered imperative by the rapid increase of the marsupials after the disappearance of their old enemies, the aborigines and the dingo. As regards the kangaroo, matters are apt to become very serious for the grazier. On an average, these animals consume as much grass as a sheep, and where a few score originally existed there soon come to be a thousand. In some places they have threatened to jostle the sheep and his master out of the land; and, in consequence, energetic and costly steps have to be taken to reduce their numbers. In a battue of this description a whole neighbourhood joins. It may seem hard that this aboriginal should be ruthlessly destroyed in favour of the sheep, because he has no wool;

but then, if he could reflect, he would see that, fed and cared for as the merino is, yet his fate would usually be the butcher at last.

The battue is not so welcome to the sportsman as the chase of the forester. The 'old man,' when finally run down, backs like a stag into a convenient corner, perhaps the hollow of a great gum-tree, the trunk of which has been partly burned away with a bush fire, and there, with a calm no-surrender expression in his mute face, and just the merest blaze in the big deer-like eyes, waits for the enemy like the splendidly resolute old veteran he is. If he can find a water-pool or river in which to 'stick up,' so much the better for him and the worse for those who attack him. He wades in until only his nervous fore-arms and head are above water, and in this position can keep even a half-dozen dogs from coming to quarters. The forester, standing six feet high, has the advantage over the dogs that, while he stands upon his hind-legs, they must swim.

Of the amphibious platypus everybody has heard. The creature has been playfully likened unto a creditor, because it is a 'beast with a bill'; but its peculiarities do not stop here. As a survival, or a 'connecting link,' it has other qualities that render it an object almost of veneration to the naturalist. It is a mammal, suckling its young, and yet it lays eggs. This fact was long known to bushmen, but it was doubted by the scientific world, and Mr. W. H. Caldwell, 'travelling bachelor,' of Cambridge, visited Australia in 1884-5, to specially study the subject, and his researches proved that, as the bushmen had declared, the platypus is oviparous. On the one hand, the platypus, with its duck's bill and its webbed feet, connects the beast with the bird, and, on the other hand, its peculiar oviparian qualities are held to establish a relationship with the reptile. The name once given it, 'water-mole,' indicates its size, though certainly the platypus has considerably the advantage of the mole. It is larger, indeed, than the largest water-rat. When the first specimens were taken to Europe a hoax, we are told, was suspected, the idea being that the bill and the feet had been cunningly attached to the body; but the platypus is too common a creature for the idea to be long entertained, and so its existence was officially acknowledged, and it received the title *Ornithorhynchus*. The platypus is a 'survival,' and it is likely to survive for many a generation. It breeds in security in a chamber at the end of a long passage which it constructs from the river banks. It is sensitive to sound, and, as it dives with alacrity, and swims with only its beak above water, a shot is no easy matter. As it is still to be obtained in streams so well visited as the Yarra and the Gippsland Avon, it may be imagined that its existence in other rivers is perfectly secure. Yet its skin is much valued. As a fur it is equal to the sealskin; and if the animal were only larger it would be systematically hunted for its covering.

Australia is rich in the abundance and variety of birds of the parrot tribe, and in the occurrence of peculiar species of the feathered race. She possesses the birds of Paradise, the king parrot, the blue mountain-parrot, the lories, parroquets and love-birds. The plumage of other birds is often of the gayest type. Thus, the blue wren is common about Nutbourne; and this bird, says Gould, is hardly surpassed by any of the feathered tribe, certainly by none but the humming-birds of America. The cockatoo, with white, black, or rosy crest, flies in flocks, and few sights in the world are prettier than one of these flights. When they finally settle on a tree, they cover it as with a snow-drift. Noisy they are, and clever, never feeding in the settled districts without posting sentinels to warn the rest of the approach of the human enemy.

THE PLATYPUS.

One of the most interesting birds of Australia is the so-called lyre-bird, the *Menura Victoria* of the naturalist, the 'pheasant' of the settler, and the 'bullard-bullard' of the aborigines, the two words somewhat resembling the native note of the graceful creature. Gould was strongly of opinion that the lyre-bird, and not the emu, should be selected as the emblem of Australia, since it is very beautiful, strictly peculiar to the country, and 'an object of the highest interest.'

The lyre-bird is about the size of the pheasant, and is valued because of the magnificent tail of the male bird. The tail is about three feet long. The outer feathers are beautifully marked, and form the lyre from which the bird takes its name. There are also curious narrow centre feathers crossing each other at the base, and curving gracefully outwards at the top. The habitat of the lyre-bird is the romantic fern country of South-eastern Australia, and the creature is in accord with its lovely surroundings. It has many

THE LYRE-BIRD.

peculiarities. Thus, the male bird forms a mound of earth, on which it promenades, displaying its tail to its utmost advantage, and uttering its liquid notes for the benefit of its female audience—for the female, dowdy as she is in comparison with her lord, has to be wooed and won. Then they are the best of mocking-birds. They imitate with precision the notes of the laughing jackass, the parrot, the solemn mopoke, and moreover they reproduce every sound made by man. Every splitter on the mountain-side has his story of endeavouring in vain to discover the users of a cross-cut saw in the neighbourhood, until he found that a 'pheasant' was mocking him; and another favourite topic is the perplexity of the 'new chum' settler, who hears an invisible mate chopping wood on his allotment, with an invisible but barking dog at his heels. The lyre-bird is slow of flight, and he would have a poor chance of escape from the shot-gun were his haunt not in the thick fern vegetation; but this jungle protects him. The birds are not so common as they once were in the ranges immediately about Melbourne, but in the fastnesses of Gippsland they are met with in their old numbers.

The satin or bower-bird is another of Australia's wonders. It not only builds a 'bower,' but decorates the structure with the most gaily-coloured articles that can be collected, such as the blue tail-feathers of the rose-bill and Pennantian parrots, bleached bones, the shells of snails, &c. Some of the feathers are stuck in among the twigs, while others, with the bones and shells, are strewed about near the entrances. The propensity of these birds to pick up and fly off with any attractive object is so well known to the natives that they always search the runs for any small missing article, such as the bowl of a pipe, that may have been accidentally dropped in the bush. In the spotted bower-bird the approaches are decorated with shells, skulls, and bones, especially those which have been bleached white by the sun; and as these birds feed almost entirely upon seeds and fruits, the shells and bones cannot have been collected for any other purpose than ornament.

Another bird peculiar to Australia is the 'giant kingfisher,' or 'piping crow,' or 'musical magpie,' or 'settler's clock,' or, to use the term everywhere applied, 'the laughing jackass.' Its extraordinary note, and insane and yet good-humoured prolonged and loud cachinnation is unique, and so is the appearance of the bird. It is a great Australian favourite, is never shot, and as a consequence is tolerant of man. It is called the 'settler's clock' in the bush by virtue of its regular hilarious uproar at noon-tide and of its far-heard 'salutation to the moon,' and it will equally make any city reserve lively with its note. A dog-show was recently held in the Melbourne Exhibition. Five hundred dogs naturally made themselves audible. But above all the discord was heard the laugh of the giant kingfisher, intimating that he had secured a golden perch from the pond, and was disposed to rejoice accordingly. It is doubtful whether the laughing jackass destroys snakes. His critics deny the assertion, which is made on his behalf. His admirers cling to a belief which is wide-spread and has earned for the jackass the immunity from destruction which he enjoys.

The largest game bird is the emu, but it is not pursued by sportsmen.

The chase is cruel, and is only indulged in by stockmen and Bohemians of the plain, who traffic in the skins, for which, unfortunately for the emu, there is a good commercial demand. Before a horse can be of any service as an emu hunter he must become accustomed to the peculiar rustling sound of the long light tail-feathers when the bird is in rapid motion. Further, he must be sound of wind and limb to keep alongside an emu; and these virtues are centred in some of the veteran stock-horses, which by long practice have become

THE GIANT KINGFISHER, OR LAUGHING JACKASS.

accustomed to tread closely upon the heels of a racer while the rider uses his long stock-whip. Swerve as the hunted animal may, the old stock-horse never leaves the line. In this way the emu is generally run down, only horse and whip being used. At first he runs with a long clean swinging stride, but as he tires the legs bend outward and get farther apart, until the movement is more akin to the waddle of a fat barn-yard goose. He struggles along bravely until every fragment of strength is gone, and then falls never to rise again.

The finest game-bird in Australia is the bustard, or wild turkey, which is found all over the continent, but more plentifully in the Western District of Victoria. On those clear frosty winter mornings peculiar to the interior

you may see them standing rigidly out in the centre of the plain, as though the

THE EMU.

cold of the night had frozen them into bird-statues. As they avoid the timber, and keep almost constantly to the open, it is only by artifice that the sportsman can get within range. For generations they have been stalked by the blacks, and have thus inherited a dread of man when on foot. They are shot without much difficulty from the saddle or a vehicle, the usual method being to drive round the bird in narrowing circles until within range.

The native companion, a bird of very much the same habits and size as the wild turkey, but very different from him in plumage and appearance, also frequents the plains, and is often found in very large flocks. Although not generally esteemed as a table bird, he sometimes finds his way into the game market, plucked and dressed, and masquerading as a turkey. An occasional blue feather beneath the wing instead of the spangled grey of the turkey now and again betrays the deception, but, as the birds at table are accepted by all except experts as being genuine wild turkeys, the difference in the flavour of the bird is not very marked.

Wild ducks are almost universal in Australia. The finest of them all is the beautiful mountain duck, found all over the continent, but which seems more closely associated with the woods and waters of Lake George, in New South Wales. On this broad sheet of water they float in countless thousands, and nest in the thickets upon its banks. Next to them in size comes the black duck, a long low bird as seen in the water, and one of the finest of Australian wild ducks. The wood-duck is, according to strict scientific classification, a diminutive goose. It has the head, bill, and body of a goose, and yet in popular estimation it is, and always will be, a wild duck, and one of the most beautifully plumaged of Australian ducks. The drakes have some of the brilliant tints of the English mallard, and the neck and head are a rich velvet brown, while the breast-feathers are beautifully spangled. The Australian teal is much larger than the English bird, but otherwise not unlike it. These four varieties are the best known, but the widgeon and blue-wing are also plentiful, and outside these are at least half a dozen varieties less familiar to Australian sportsmen.

The black swan can hardly be called a game bird, but it is shot on all the lakes and swamps along the southern coast. In the Gippsland lakes it is not an uncommon thing to find thousands of swans in a single flock, and when these rise for a flight, striking the water with feet and wings, the noise can be heard for miles across the lake. When means have been taken to get rid of a rather rank flavour, just as the taste of the gum-leaves is removed from opossum flesh, the swan is occasionally eaten as game. Both swans and ducks are very largely shot from light punts, and for many years punt and swivel guns were used with terrible destruction by men whose business it was to supply the game markets of the large cities. In Victoria the Legislature has by enactment declared the swivel gun an illegal instrument, and since its abolition the ducks are returning in hundreds to their old breeding-grounds.

Smaller game is abundant everywhere. The snipe, as nearly as possible a prototype of the British bird, provides good shooting, more especially in Gippsland. British epicures would be shocked at the uses to which the bird is put in rough bush cookery, where its virtues are held in small esteem. An Irish recipe for cooking a snipe is merely to burn its bill in a candle, but some Australian cooks go to the other extreme. One recipient of a present of a few brace 'just fried them with steak.' The heresy as regards the steak was bad enough, but such treatment of snipe was altogether unpardonable. The Argus snipe is a rare but rather beautiful bird, the markings on its back and wings being exceptionally fine. Of Australian quail there are at least a dozen varieties, ranging from a small partridge down to the little king quail. In some parts of the colony, without the slightest efforts being made at game preservation, enormous bags are frequently made.

THE TIGER-SNAKE.

Amongst the game of southern forests the wonga-wonga and bronze-wing pigeons are two really splendid birds, the latter as large as an ordinary blue-rock, and the former making all varieties of the pigeon tribe look like mere dwarfs beside them. They keep closely to the thickets. It requires a quick eye to detect them.

Snakes are often considered a drawback in Australia, but then it must be remembered that a man may live ten years in a snaky part of the country and never see one of these reptiles. Now that rational ideas of treatment are gaining ground, death from snake-bites will not average above one per million of the population per annum.

The most vicious as well as the most dangerous of these reptiles is the tiger-snake, so called from its tawny, cross-banded colouring. Like its near ally, the cobra di capello of India, when irritated it flattens and extends its neck to twice its natural size. A full-sized tiger-snake in the summer season, when it secretes its maximum amount of poison, can inject a dose that is speedily fatal.

The treatment in snake-bite cases is still in dispute. The Indian doctors reject ammonia, and are followed by the Central Board of Health (Victoria), which has issued notices recommending excision and the use of the ligature. Spirits are given in abundance by some medical men. Walking the sufferer about to avert sleep and coma is a popular procedure. It is the general use of the excision treatment, however, that has reduced the death-rate so wonderfully. If a schoolboy is bitten now he pulls out his knife and excises the bitten part, or he sacrifices the joint of a finger. Keep the poison out of the system, and no harm is possible, and the bitten person now directs his energies to carry out that, instead of wasting his time in running after a doctor, who cannot repair the neglect.

One sport there is in Australia which can be most heartily enjoyed by all. This is shark-catching. The shark is a worse terror than the snake. Every harbour contains some monsters fourteen, sixteen, and eighteen feet long, and every year there is some tale of horror. The catching of one of these creatures is a popular event, men rejoicing over the destruction of a dreaded enemy.

To the angler Australian waters offer great attractions. Trout were long ago established in the streams of Tasmania and New Zealand, and within the last few years they have become very plentiful in Victorian rivers. Within twenty miles of Melbourne good trout-fishing may now be had. The fish are slightly more sluggish than in British waters—a fact no doubt accounted for by the warmer climate; and experts say that at table something is lost in flavour also. The Californian salmon have also been acclimatised with fair success. There are several varieties of perch in the colonies; but those of the Gippsland rivers, discarding the traditions of their kind all the world over, rise eagerly to the fly, and give splendid sport. To kill fifty a day with the fly, many of them going up to five pounds, is not an uncommon feat. The bream in all the southern rivers and lakes are strong, lusty fellows, that make the reels whistle in a style that is sweetest music to the angler's ear; but if one wants a bag, he must use double-gutted hooks. Gamer or better fish than these bream no fisherman could desire. The triton of Australian sweet-water streams is the Murray cod; but he has nothing but his size to recommend him. Along the coast and in the tidal rivers the so-called sea-salmon is another source of gratification to the fly-fisher, for he rises freely, and the largest ones make quite a gallant rush when struck. In the lagoons bordering on the chief of Australian rivers, there are large Murray perch that at certain times bite voraciously. But the handsomest of his kind in Australia is undoubtedly the golden perch, found in the Murray and its tributaries. Its scales have the beautiful burnished gleam of old gold, and when a big one is brought to bank it is something to admire. Judged from the standard of the epicure alone, the black-fish is perhaps the finest of all Australian fresh-water fish, its flesh being snow-white, and of a remarkably fine flavour. The fish is found to greatest perfection in the clear mountain streams that come tumbling down from the Otway ranges, in the southern part of Victoria; but he is of sluggish habits, and by no means the angler's ideal. When these streams are discoloured by storm water very good fishing may be had through the day; but if the water is clear the black-fish comes from his hiding-place only when the shadows from the hill-tops begin to deepen over the water.

In some few rivers widening into the sea whiting are caught at certain periods of the year. The best sea-fishing is perhaps that to be had with the schnapper in Port Phillip Bay, where the fish are plentiful about the lines of reef, and range in weight up to forty pounds. Notwithstanding the merits of some of the native fish, the traditional love for trout has risen superior to every other inclination with the anglers of Victoria and Tasmania. The trout in many places have worked themselves so far up the streams that man can only follow with the greatest difficulty, and the scrub is so thick that an angler would find it hopeless to attempt a cast. With these natural preserves extending for miles, the supply of trout in colonial rivers is inexhaustible. In fly-fishing for trout in the colonies it has been found, however, that the most sacredly observed rules of British angling are entirely useless. Flies that were deadly in the old country are impotent here; and, as far as the Australian is concerned, all the main tenets of the fly-fisher's faith must be absolutely cast aside, and a new angling creed built upon the basis of colonial insect life and the changed habits of the trout as we know them in Australia.

Australian vegetation is sometimes considered monotonous in appearance. But this is the criticism of the stranger, and not of the resident. The first idea of the observer is one of uniformity. When the Chinese originally came to Australia, no one could see any difference between the units of the Mongolian horde. Often did robbers of fowl-houses escape punishment from the inability of the prosecutor to identify the men he had chased and lost sight of, and frequently, it is to be feared, was the wrong wearer of the pigtail stoutly sworn to. The yellow skin, the round face and the flat nose conveyed the idea of identity. And to Chinamen all Europeans were alike. The puzzled Celestial could not distinguish between Englishman and German, and still less between individual beef-eaters.

But Australian vegetation has distinctive features that quickly catch the eye. The eucalypt is always the eucalypt, with its sombre green and its peculiar adjustment of foliage. The leaves do not spread out horizontally, but depend vertically from the boughs, an arrangement which minimises the shade afforded in the daytime, but gives beautiful effects in the gloaming, when the tree, not obscuring the light, becomes a network of elegant tracery. Viewed in the daytime in juxtaposition to oak or elm, and the confession must be made that the average gum of the plains is scraggy; but in the moonlight the oak or elm will be a black blotch, when the eucalypt is transformed into a wonder of light and shade and of graceful outlines. An acquaintance with the bush soon dispels the notion of monotony. The eucalypts are found to differ one from another; the handsome Banksias, the curious Casuarinas, or shea-oaks, the graceful acacias, all claim attention and individualise the scene, while palms, grass-trees and tree-ferns add charm and character to many a landscape.

In vegetation as in other matters Australia delights in the vast, sometimes in the *outré*, often in the contrast of extremes. Dwarf scrub will cover whole regions. One tract of the mallee scrub, shared between Victoria and South Australia, covers an area of nearly 9000 square miles. The mallee is just high enough to render it impossible for a man on horseback to look over it. And on the mountain ranges in the same colony are to be found long stretches and avenues of the 'giant gums,' whose pure white silvery columns seem as though intended to support the sky. Between these two extremes is to be found a pleasantly-wooded country presenting a park-like appearance. Farther afield are the interior plains, covered often with the terrible spinifex, or porcupine grass, a hard, coarse and spiny grass,

AUSTRALIAN TREES.

uneatable by horse or ass, or, I believe, by camel, and apt to wound the feet of the unfortunate animal that journeys over it.

Different indeed from these treeless, waterless steppes are the valleys and mountains of the seaboard. In these regions, protected from hot winds and favoured by a heavy rainfall, we have a luxuriant and elegant vegetation. Beginning with the gullies of the Dandenong ranges, near Melbourne, the traveller can proceed from fairy scene to fairy scene along the coast to far-away Carpentaria and Papua, the vegetation preserving its identity, and yet slowly changing from a sub-tropical to a tropical character. In the Victorian region there are rivulets of clear water hidden from sight by the tree-ferns which flourish on their banks. Journeying northwards, the vegetation thickens. Parasitical ferns—the staghorns of the conservatory—depend from every branch. Palm-trees make their appearance, the noble *Livistonia* attaining in suitable places a height of eighty feet. The musk-tree and the *Pittosporum* scent the air, and lovely twining plants help to form an impenetrable foliage. On reaching the ranges of New South Wales, the luxuriance is found to have further developed. From some hill-top you gaze upon a verdant lawn gay with flowers and studded with shrubs. Descending, you find that the surface is a vegetable canopy formed by stout and hardy creepers and climbers that spread from tree to tree, only the tops of the lofty eucalypts appearing above this mid-air canopy. Lower down, fern-trees and cabbage-palms form a second roof, while the soil supports an undergrowth of mosses, lichens and ferns.

But the gum-tree is as distinctive of Australia as are the emu and the kangaroo. It pleases Australians greatly that their country contains the 'tallest tree in the world.' For years it was believed that Nature had done her utmost in the big trees of California, but experts and visitors admit that this belief must be abandoned. The two countries have the issue to themselves; but the *Sequoia gigantea* has had to retire in favour of the *Eucalyptus amygdalina*, or giant gum. The following list of generally accepted heights will show how completely the indigenous vegetation of other lands is put out of court :—

The elm	60 feet to 80 feet.
The oak	60 feet to 100 feet.
Pinus insignis	60 feet to 100 feet.
Himalayan cedar	200 feet.
Sequoia gigantea, or 'big tree' of California	200 feet to 325 feet.
Eucalyptus amygdalina, or giant gum . .	250 feet to 480 feet.

The giant gum is rich in a peculiar volatile oil, and it supplies a splendid timber for shingles, palings, &c. Hence, in all accessible parts, the fine specimens are doomed to early destruction by the splitter. The woodman does *not* spare the tree. The more huge the round, straight, polished, and beautiful stem, the more likely he is to mark it as his own. Confident statements have been made that in favoured spots the giant gum attains the height of 500 feet; just as equally confident assertions have been published that the *Sequoia* of California runs up to 450 feet. The highest gum of which there is authentic record is growing on Mount Baw-Baw, Gippsland. Mr. Clement Hodgkinson, C.E., gives the official measurement as 471 feet. The highest tree now standing in California is 325 feet, so that the eucalypt is the taller by 146 feet. If two tall elms, 70 feet high, were placed on the top of the tallest *Sequoia* in existence, the Mount Baw-Baw eucalypt would still overlook the three.

The Fernshaw or Black Spur timber is famous because it is easily reached from Melbourne, but the trees themselves are not the head of their clan. A gum felled in the Otway ranges, at the instance of the late Professor Wilson, measured 378 feet to the spot where its top had been broken off, and, allowing for the average taper, 40 feet had been carried away. A gum felled at Dandenong, and measured by Mr. D. Boyle, measured 420 feet. And the quantity of the timber supported by the soil where these large trees are found is very remarkable. The secretary of the State Forest Board noted the growth on one acre of ground in the Upper Yarra district, and he found that the plot contained twenty eucalypts of a height of 350 feet, and thirty-eight saplings of a height of 50 feet, these trees emerging from a dense undergrowth of fern and musk trees.

In his *Goldfields of Victoria* Mr. Brough Smith photographs a tree 69 feet in circumference, and 330 feet in height, and of greater proportions therefore than the greatest of the *Sequoias*. This tree, with hundreds of others, was felled for splitting purposes. The Australian giants abound, and new discoveries are constantly made; and it is quite possible that in some one of the valleys yet to be broken into by man the real giant of the globe will be discovered. The picture on page 16 of the Gippsland railway running through a cleared track gives some idea of a primæval forest in Victoria.

Mention has been made of the silver columns of the giant gum. The tree sheds its bark annually, and the new skin is of a pure and dazzling whiteness. As the stem is perfectly cylindrical, and as the huge fabric towers 200 and 250 feet high without a branch, the sight of a group of these monarchs is at these times especially beautiful. Below are the tree-ferns and a lovely bush undisturbed by the wind, which may be heard rustling the far-off tops of the grove. The elegant lyre-birds will be drinking at a spring. Parrots of gorgeous plumage flit by. Few can gaze upon such a scene without emotion, without realising with silent awe that this fair spot is Nature's temple. And then the oppressed heart, acknowledging the charm, will turn from all that Nature gives to what she must bring.

Of the other gums the pride of place must be awarded to the noble *Ecalpytus rostrata*, or red gum of the colonists. Fine specimens are still to be found near Melbourne, though the value of its wood has marked them out for destruction in the neighbourhood of towns and cities. The *Rostrata* has an enormous spreading upper growth. Some of the limbs rival in size the parent stem, and will be gnarled and contorted in a manner recalling the writhings of the Laocoon. It should be studied from a distance, for their enormous weight sometimes causes the branches to snap suddenly without the slightest warning, to the ruin of all below.

The rival of the red gum as a timber tree is the jarrah, an eucalypt peculiar to Western Australia, where it grows in forests. Seen in its home on the Darling range, or

the hills of Geographe Bay, the jarrah is a magnificent tree, running up to a hundred feet before it branches, and reminding the spectator sometimes of the rostrata, and sometimes of the giant gum. The specialty of the jarrah is its power to defy the ravages of the insect world and of the sea. This is complete. An examination recently made of a pier at Banjoewangie, which was constructed thirty years ago of jarrah, showed that the piles were as sound as the day they were put in, although the seas of Java swarm with the *Teredo navalis*. The official examination made by a select committee of Parliament in South Australia, in 1870, of the Port Adelaide bridge, erected in 1858, disclosed the fact that while every other timber employed below water 'had been completely destroyed by the teredo and other submarine insects, the jarrah remained unscathed,' and had apparently saved the work from collapse. In point of beauty many award the palm amongst the gums to the *Eucalyptus ficifolia*, or scarlet flowering gum. It is met with in groups. The tufts of bright scarlet blossom contrast well with the dark-green foliage, and the tree adds greatly to the attraction of the West Australian bush.

The mallee (*Eucalyptus dumosa*) is one of the strangest products of a strange country. The root is a globular mass, varying in size from a child's head to a huge mass which a man can hardly carry. From this bulb a tap root descends to a great depth to reach moist ground below, while other roots spread more horizontally. Above ground a few saplings shoot out to a maximum height of about twenty feet, each sapling having a tuft of leaves at its top. The appearance is that of a skeleton umbrella, with the central stick or handle removed. No surface water is to be obtained in the mallee district; its silence is only disturbed by the melancholy wail of the dingo. Miserable is the fate of the luckless wretch who wanders into such tracts as these. Unable to discern his way, or to gain any point of vantage, and suffering from thirst, the man's reason often succumbs, and he perishes a maniac. Yet the Victorian mallee district is now being cleared by energetic colonists, who aver that when they have exterminated the rabbit, and poisoned the dingo, and got rid of the scrub—which succumbs to treatment —these plains will prove the most fertile in Australia.

Here allusion may be made to the question whether or not the eucalyptus is a fever-destroying tree. The subject has been thoroughly investigated and discussed by Mr. Joseph Bosisto, M.P., Commissioner for Victoria at the Colonial and Indian Exhibition, 1886, and his decision is in favour of the utility of the eucalypt. Mr. Bosisto dwells specially upon the fact that malarious diseases are not native to Australia, and that imported fevers are believed to diminish in virulence; and he directly connects the absence of malarious disease with the presence of a peculiar aroma-diffusing vegetation. Mr. Bosisto mentions the powerful root action of the eucalyptus, which, being an evergreen, is continually at work, absorbing humidity from the earth, and upon its large leaf exudation of oil and acid. His contention is that the volatile oil thrown off by the eucalyptus absorbs atmospheric oxygen, and transforms it into ozone. This much is certain : that if a small quantity of any of the eucalyptus oils be sprinkled in a sick room, the pleasure of breathing an improved air is realised at once. And as Mr. Bosisto contends that he has established the diffusion of volatile oil by the eucalyptus, and the chemical consequences of such diffusion, he submits with a calm confidence that 'there is an active agency in Australian vegetation unknown in other countries,' and that the eucalyptus is rightly described as an anti-fever tree.

The tree most favoured for this purpose is the blue gum, or *Eucalyptus globus*. The blue gum is extensively cultivated outside of Australia, because experiment shows that it produces the most timber in the least time. The rapidity with which the Australian forest recovers itself after apparent destruction is indeed one of its marvels. In conversation a landed proprietor of Benambra mentioned how, twenty-five years back, there were places in his district in which scarce a stick could be seen—then diggers had cut down every tree for firewood and for their workings. But the diggers have gone, and now there is again the original dense forest.

Next to the eucalypt the tree most prized in Australia is the graceful acacia, varieties of which flourish throughout the continent. The tall slender stem of the 'wattle'—as the tree is termed—supporting a feathery foliage is everywhere to be met with in the south-eastern colonies. In the spring-time the valleys and their river-courses are lit up with the golden bloom which the tree bears in rare profusion, and the perfume scents the air. In a room the odour of a mere twig of the wattle will often be found to be overpowering. In England the young people can 'go a-Maying,' and in Australia they have no happier time than when they go 'to bring the wattle home.' The quotation is the refrain of a song which the sentiment made popular. Not only is the wattle 'a thing of beauty' in itself, but the circumstance that its bark is one of the most powerful tanning agencies in the world, and has a high commercial value accordingly, renders it to its possessor 'a joy for ever.' The tree is now being extensively planted in Victoria, where the valuable varieties flourish, not by landscape gardeners, but by shrewd agriculturists intent upon netting £10 per ton from the bark.

A world of other vegetation demands notice. The seaboard has a characteristic shrub of its own in the so-called tea-tree scrub, described by Baron von Mueller as a 'myrtle-like *Leptospermum*, of tall stature, with half-snowy, half-rosy flowers.' It is the best of sand-binders. No tract is so inhospitable but that the tea-tree will flourish there. It fights the ocean to its edge. On some jutting promontory on which not a rush will grow, exposed to every storm and swept by spray, the tea-tree will be found, stunted and deserted, but still battling bravely for existence against sea and breeze.

Inland the shea-oak (*Casuarina striata*) attracts attention. It is scattered over the continent, and once seen is always remembered. The tree is well shaped, but is leafless, long thin thongs taking the place of foliage. The dark and gloomy appearance of the tree impresses itself upon the spectator, and so, if he camps near it at night, does the melancholy moaning of the wind through its pendent whip-like branchlets.

Small space has been left for a notice of such marvels as the bottle-tree, and such beauties of Australian vegetation as the flame-tree. The Sydney or Queensland visitor in the summer season may see in full bloom, in the

THE BOTTLE-TREE.

Illawarra bush, the local 'flame-tree' (*Sterculia acerifolia*). The tree bears a profusion of scarlet racemes of flowers, and of large bright green leaves. The foliage sheds itself to make room for the profuse inflorescence, so that the tree has veritably the appearance of a fire. Cycads and palm-lilies are picturesque wherever they are met with.

The grass-trees (*Xanthorrhœa*) are peculiar to Australia, and in some places cover myriads of acres. I have seen them in valleys in Western Australia growing so thickly that it was impossible to push a horse through their ranks. A rugged resinous stem five to ten feet high supports a drooping plume of wiry foliage, from which a flowering bulrush springs. The 'black boy,' as the grass-tree is called in the west, is often weird, and is essentially Australian. Useful advice to a settler would be, 'Be chary of buying land where the grass-tree grows,' for, though there are exceptions, the *Xanthorrhœa* has a weakness for the desert. The warratah, with its single stem of six feet, bearing a crimson blossom resembling a full-blown peony, is one of the most popular of the wild flowers of New South Wales. The boronia, with its powerful perfume, will be admired by the visitor; the *Araucarias* have here their home. The heaths are beautiful; and it may be said of them in their place and season, 'You scarce can see the grass for flowers.' For a long time the wild flowers of the country were neglected, but now in some places shows are exclusively devoted to them. The dictum of Mr. A. A. Wallace is not to be lightly challenged, and it is that 'no country in the world affords a greater variety of lovely flowers than Australia, nor more interesting forms of vegetable life.'

The grape is providing us with a national industry; the orange-groves of Sydney, Perth, and other districts are amongst the sights of the place.

GRASS-TREES.

DRIVING CATTLE.

CHAPTER XIII.

THE SQUATTER AND THE SETTLER.

PRESENT MEANING OF THE WORD 'SQUATTER'—CATTLE-RAISING—CAPITAL HAS CONFIDENCE IN SQUATTING NOW—ORIGIN OF MERINO SHEEP-BREEDING—MANAGEMENT OF A RUN—DROUGHT—BOX-TREE CLEARINGS—MODERN ENTERPRISE—SHEEP-SHEARING—'SUNDOWNERS'—FARMING PROSPECTS—CHEAP LAND—EASY HARVESTING—SMALL CAPITAL—SELECTION CONDITIONS—BUSH FIRES—BLACK THURSDAY—THE OTWAY DISASTER—LOST IN THE BUSH—MISSING CHILDREN.

THE terms 'squatter' and 'squatting' are now misleading. They cover a number of different occupations, and perhaps the words 'grazier' and 'grazing' ought to be substituted. The original squatter paid his £10 licence fee, and he was at liberty to go where he pleased and to take up as much land as he required for his sheep and for two years' increase. Whether he had five hundred sheep or five thousand did not matter. Australia was large, and the adventurous pioneer was at liberty to pick and choose. The flocks were 'shepherded'—that is, were not confined between fences, but were looked after by men who drove them to their feed during the day, and placed them inside hurdles at head-quarters at night. But, as land was taken up, the squatter obtained a particular run for a term of years. He subdivided it by fences into paddocks, and so reduced his number of herds and conducted his operations more scientifically.

When a new run is taken up, it is pretty sure, in the first instance, to be stocked with cattle. Cattle-raising requires no heavy outlay of capital, because, beyond horses for the men, yards to work the stock, and perhaps one or two paddocks to enclose young heifers and separate them from the general herd, no buildings have to be erected. Then the produce of a cattle station—the fat stock—can be cheaply driven to market. Travelling with stock through the bush costs no more than the wages of the men employed, and, if carefully driven, the bullocks do not deteriorate. Last but not least among the advantages possessed by the cattle squatter is the fact that he can make shift with comparatively few water-holes. Cattle can feed their way to water much more readily than sheep.

At first cattle are not happy on a new country, and will make frequent efforts to break away. Often have the stockmen left a herd quietly grazing at night, and found not a hoof in the morning, whereupon comes a fine gallop after the runaways, who always head straight for home. Nevertheless skilful herding of the cattle on the run, and extra vigilance for a few months, suffice to accustom the animals to their new home. Once 'broken in to the run,' as it is called, the cattle remain on it, and can indeed hardly be driven away. They select their camps—generally tracts of open country, with trees growing in groups, and near water—and the choice is often directed by the stockmen when first they are brought on to the country. On these camps the cattle assemble in the heat of the day, lying lazily in the shade, and moving off to feed at night and in the afternoon and morning. They are easily trained to assemble on the camp whenever hunted up, and the crack of a stock-whip anywhere on a cattle-run, with a well-broken herd, will set all the animals within hearing moving off to the camp. Mustering is attended to at frequent intervals on a well-worked cattle station. The stockmen ride round, hunting up all stray groups, and direct them to the central camp, where they assemble in a great compact herd. When thus gathered together, the animals required for any special purpose—fat bullocks for market, or cows and calves for branding—are ridden out of the mass by the stockmen on their well-trained horses, and collected in a separate herd.

There is no more interesting sight than this 'cutting out,' as it is called. The stockman rides into the mass of animals, which opens out uneasily as he enters. A touch of the stock-whip on the selected beast indicates him to the intelligent horse, whose rider practically leaves to him the rest of the work. The selected beast tries to escape by wedging himself into masses of his companions; but the horse, who apparently enters thoroughly into the fun of the thing, turns and twists with surprising rapidity, and, before the hunted animal knows what is happening to him, he finds himself edged outside of the main herd, and driven to a separate little group. Other men guard this group, and prevent them from rejoining the mass, plying their stock-whips with terrible effect on any refractory beast. When the selection is complete, the chosen herd is driven towards the head station yards, and the main body of cattle allowed to disperse again.

Cattle-raising is a pursuit full of excitement and danger. Chasing the wild animals through the bush or down the steep sides of precipitous hills is work that requires sure feet on the part of the horse, and cool heads and firm seats on the part of the riders. Even more perilous is drafting in the yards. The men who enter the great enclosures full of angry frightened animals, to separate and drive them into different compartments, often run quite as much risk as the Spanish bull-fighters. But they have quick feet, sharp eyes, and cool heads, and fatal accidents seldom occur; though it often happens that a charging cow or bullock will send all the men in the yard scrambling precipitately to the top rail of the strong high timber enclosure.

Drought is the great enemy that these pioneers have to dread. Nature has fitted the grasses and herbage of the interior to withstand prolonged dry periods. By many beautiful adaptations the herbs growing on the plain are enabled to flower and mature their seed with great rapidity; so that even one soaking downpour will often suffice for the lifetime of a plant, and allow it to shed its ripened seed, which lies hidden in the cracks of the arid, sun-baked soil till the next favourable season occurs. The principal grasses have a remarkable power of remaining in what seems like a state of suspended animation. This is especially noticeable in the case of the Mitchell grass, which becomes white and apparently dead, but still retains nourishment for stock in its dried leaves, and vitality in its apparently withered stems.

One great reason why the squatter is better off now than he ever was before is that capital has confidence in the occupation. Thus the individual is more secure than he was. And large institutions have been formed that make it their business to finance for the squatter. These institutions have their one, two, or three millions of English and Scotch capital, and they are managed by men of great colonial experience, who know it is bad policy to do other than support a deserving pioneer right through. Their capital is indeed subscribed for the purpose of making stations drought-proof, and their record shows that the system is highly profitable. An enormous amount of the annexation of the desert which is now going on has English and Scotch gold as its basis; and this union of home capital and of colonial enterprise is as happy and as effectual a form of federation as can be desired.

The following remarks on squatting are contributed by Mr. G. A. Brown, author of the standard work, *Sheep Breeding in Australia*: 'It is curious that the first settlers in Australia firmly believed the country to be quite unfitted for rearing wool-bearing sheep. For fully a quarter of a century the hairy sheep of India and the Cape of Good Hope were bred by the colonists; and it was not till Captain McArthur sold Australian grown merino wool in the London market at the rate of 5s. per lb., that the sheep-owners became aware of the splendid industry that awaited development. Merino sheep then became the rage, and large sums of money were spent in importing the finest specimens of the breed from the purest flocks in Germany. In a few years Australia took her place at the head of the list of fine wool-producing countries, and has held it ever since. The world never before saw merino wool so soft, so bright, or so long in staple. It produced a revolution in the manufacture of woollen fabrics, and it brought within the reach of the artisan cloths of a quality that only the wealthy could afford in the previous century. This great work has been effected by the Australian squatters.

A MERINO SHEEP.

The management of live-stock in the old squatting days was thoroughly patriarchal. The sheep were kept in flocks varying from 800 to 2000 head, according to the character of the country, tended all day by shepherds, and inclosed at night in hurdle yards. As a further protection against lurking blackfellow or prowling dingo, a man slept in a small wooden portable cabin, called a watch-box, close by the sheep. It was no uncommon thing for the men to be roused up two or three times during the night; but, as they had plenty of time to sleep during the day, this was thought no great hardship. The shepherds led an inexpressibly dreary life; they were out at daybreak, and, having turned their sheep in the proper direction, they followed them all day, seldom exchanging a word with a human being till they returned to the hut at night. Many of them became eccentric, or, as the working bushmen called it, "cranky," and were quite unfit for any other occupation. As the stock increased, the whole flock could not be fed from the home station, round which the grass was usually reserved for the horses and working bullocks; huts were then erected from three to ten miles or even farther away, according to the size of the station or run, as the leaseholds were called. At these huts, known as out-stations, generally two flocks of sheep were kept, a hut-keeper being employed to cook for the shepherds and shift the hurdle yards every day, so that the sheep might have a clean bed.

'In the old days the country was all unenclosed from one end to the other. Vehicles were scarce—there were few coaches, and occasionally a gig would be seen on a main road. The ordinary mode of travelling through the country was on horseback. On arriving at a station the usual plan was to ride up to the principal hut, ask for the proprietor, and announce your name; an invitation to stay all night followed as a matter of course. Hospitality was a duty that was most religiously performed by almost every squatter. There were a few exceptions, and they were branded with the prefix of "hungry" attached to their names, and, being known, were avoided alike by horsemen and footmen.

'Improvements in bush life were being steadily made when the discovery of gold brought the country prominently under the notice of European countries. The old pastoral life, with all its rustic charm and quietude, disappeared as thoroughly as if it had never been. In the rush and turmoil that ensued many of the old squatters were ruined, while others, more lucky, succeeded in making immense fortunes. Over the greater portion of Victoria and a considerable area of New South Wales the land has been converted into freeholds, and squatting is confined to Queensland, and the vast sultry plains of Northern, Central and Western Australia. In these countries the areas held under leasehold from the Crown are of immense size, many of them being capable of carrying 300,000 sheep in good seasons. These great runs are all fenced in and subdivided by wire fences. The sheep are run in paddocks often containing over 20,000 acres. As there are few watercourses the stock are watered by means of immense excavations, called tanks, containing an area of 10,000 cubic yards of water when filled. Large as they are many of them were dried up by the long drought of 1885 and 1886. The result has been that the holders of these great pastoral properties have suffered heavy losses. I passed by one cattle station in Queensland, four years ago, on which 60,000 head of cattle were grazing. Since then, so severe has been the drought, the stock has been reduced by deaths from starvation to 20,000 head. The deaths of stock on the sheep stations in the same district have been equally heavy. When the seasons have a fair average rainfall in these hot districts everything goes well, and squatting is the most profitable occupation in the colonies, but when a series of dry years set in the squatter's lot is a heartrending one. He can do nothing for the poor creatures he sees slowly starving to death, while overhead, month after month—ay, and year after year—there is the cruel clear sky and the bright hot sun steadily withering up all life. The birds and wild animals die in thousands, and the few that still live are so feeble that their wild nature seems gone out of them. This last drought is not an exceptional event. Since Central and Northern Australia have been known, the country has suffered from periodical droughts; but every year the skill of the squatter is exercised in providing fresh supplies of water for his stock, and that is the great requisite in this climate. Given a good supply of water, and it is wonderful what a little food will keep sheep alive on the plains of Central Australia. I have seen sheep in excellent condition on country that to all appearance was absolutely bare of grass. A stranger would not believe that any animal could support life on such scanty pastures.

'Under the new order of things that followed the discovery of gold many large freehold estates were put together by the old squatters, and then it was found that a different style of management was required to make the properties pay interest on the capital expended on them. The runs were fenced and subdivided, dams were constructed on the watercourses, and where the country was too flat for dams tanks were made for supplying the stock with water. Good houses were built, and fine gardens and pleasure-grounds formed. As the proprietors of these estates became wealthy, they erected houses that for size, style and convenience would rival the pleasant homes of the country gentlemen of England. Often in a country that a score of years ago was considered a remote district in the back country, one will now meet with a handsome mansion surrounded by extensive gardens, pleasure-grounds and plantations. Where in the old squatting days water was often very scarce, there is now ample to irrigate a garden, and indeed water is usually laid on all over the modern squatter's establishment.

'Over a large area of New South Wales and Victoria the surface of the country was covered by a dense forest of the eucalypt called the box-tree. They were of medium size, and their timber was of little or no value. Having surface roots, they robbed the soil of all substance, and the result was that the box-forest country was always bare of grass. It was noticed by a few observant bushmen that the soil in these forests was excellent, and a few experiments were made in the way of clearing the land. The result was satisfactory, but felling the trees was too expensive to practise on a large scale, while the stumps were very apt to throw up a number of vigorous shoots that did as much harm as the parent tree. What use to make of the box-forest country was a puzzle, and most people regarded it as worthless. At this time a firm of squatters astonished their neighbours by purchasing a block of 20,000 acres of box-forest, at £1 per acre, that the

Surveyor-General of the colony declared was not worth 2s. 6d. per acre. The plan they adopted for killing the box-trees was one that had only lately been tried. It consisted in cutting a notch round the tree through the bark and into the sap wood, to prevent the sap rising. This plan, called 'ring barking,' when performed at the proper season, effectually kills the tree, and it has since come into general practice all over Australia. I have ridden over the estate in the box-forest that was formed by the squatting firm mentioned, and where, years ago, there was not a blade of grass to be seen, is now a fine pasture, that even in indifferent years will keep a sheep to the acre.

RING BARKING.

'Drought does not always ruin the squatter, and there are many instances of their surviving the hard time. A squatter of my acquaintance embarked in a heavy purchase in Central Australia. The run was of vast size, and the soil admirable, but soon after he purchased the property a severe drought set in, water was scarce, and grass almost entirely disappeared. There was no disposing of a portion of the sheep, for every one was short of grass, and there were no buyers. Before the drought broke up he had lost eighty thousand sheep from starvation, and the remainder of the flock were in a very emaciated condition. At last the welcome rain set in—not in a heavy shower, but in a continued downfall that lasted for several days. Such an ample rain at that time of the year meant abundance of food and water for the next twelve months. The squatter was a man of quick perception and prompt to act in an emergency. His station was in telegraphic communication with Melbourne, and, knowing how to operate, he purchased through the stock agents about ninety thousand ewes to lamb from the best flocks in the country. The story is told that he walked up and down his verandah watching the rainfall, and as each successive inch was registered over a certain point he telegraphed to Melbourne to purchase ten thousand more sheep. He got the season's lambing and the fleece from the sheep he bought, and then sold the greater portion for nearly double what he paid for them a few months before. That splendid rain made all the difference between ruin and wealth.

'Sheep-farming is carried on everywhere in Australia, while squatting on Crown lands, as we have said, is confined to the vast area of Central Australia and Western Australia. The shearing on one of the great stations in the interior is a most important operation, there being a small army of men employed while it lasts. Some of the wool-sheds are of great extent, and provide shelter for seven thousand sheep. I have seen as many as a hundred shearers at work at once. They work very hard, and earn a considerable amount of money during the season. They form bands of from forty to eighty men, and start in Queensland in July, gradually working their way south. During shearing-time the wool-shed presents a very busy and interesting scene. A hundred shearers are all working as if for a wager, for the element of rivalry enters largely into the work; a dozen half-clad blacks, male and female, are picking up the fleeces and carrying them to the wool tables, where they are skirted, rolled up, sorted and thrown into their several bins. Immediately behind the wool-bins are the presses, in which the wool is packed into bales, and at the rear the waggons are loading with bales for the distant railway station. Outside the shed men are engaged in branding the sheep after each man's work has been counted from his yard.

'The waggons load heavily, and have often teams of twenty bullocks each, while there are always a few spare bullocks travelling loose to be used as required, when one of the team gets a sore neck or knocks up. The carriers form a distinct class in the back country. They generally travel in bands of four or six teams, which are often owned by one man, who generally accompanies the caravan in a buggy, or, if unable to afford that comfort, drives one of the teams.

'A peculiar feature in station life in Australia is the existence of a class of wanderers known as "swagmen," or "sundowners," who wander over the face of the country under the pretence that they are looking for work; but they seldom accept it when offered. They lead a lazy, careless life, making for the shelter of some station towards the close of the day, when they go through the formula of asking for work, after which follows the usual inquiry for accommodation for the night. On some stations these men are such a nuisance that huts are put up for their accommodation; and, instead of permitting them to mingle with the men at their meals, they are given a certain quantity of flour, and sometimes meat. During the day they camp by the side of a creek where there is shelter from the sun, whence they do not stir till it is time to start for the station where they intend passing the night, timing their arrival about sunset. Once a man becomes a " sundowner " he is useless for any honest employment.

'The life of a successful squatter is a very pleasant one, with a large freehold estate in a settled part of the country, and an extensive mansion in which to entertain his friends, he can pass a few months very enjoyably in the country; but his real home is in one of the most aristocratic suburbs of Melbourne or Sydney, where he lives in a house that cost fully five times the value of his squatting run in the old pioneer days. The pioneers deserve rest and prosperity. They did good work in their day, and their successors are emulating their example in the great sultry plains of Central Australia.'

In due course everywhere the Australian squatter gives way to the agriculturist. The sheep become a secondary agent to the plough. In place of the squatter we have the 'selector.' Land is not given away by the state in Australia to the immigrant, and yet it is unusually easy—even for a new country—for the poor man to start farming. This remark is made on the authority of Mr. T. K. Dow, the agricultural 'special' of the *Australasian* newspaper, with whom the writer conversed on the subject for the purposes of this volume. Mr. Dow had just returned to the colonies after a tour through America, made for the purpose of procuring information on agricultural matters, and he could thus speak as an expert. He says :—

'In Australia a man selects a piece of land; he pays the survey fee, and then he pays for the fee-simple by annual instalments. But nearly all the land so selected is fit for the plough. The man gets a crop off it the very first year, so that he can pay his way as he goes. The land you get for nothing in other countries is worth nothing in the first instance. It has to be made valuable. There are expensive improvements that have to be effected, and so you want more money to start with there than you do in Australia. It is surprising with how little capital men do start here.

'The Australian harvesting system is the cheapest in the world, and is peculiar to the country. There is a dryness about the crops of the northern plains, on which the bulk of the wheat in South Australia and Victoria is grown, and this enables the "stripper" to be used. The stripper is an Australian invention. It is described by its name. It squeezes the corn out, and leaves the stalk standing. The corn is threshed upon the straw, and the straw is afterwards burnt off or is ploughed in.'

Mr. Dow is an enthusiastic irrigationist, and it is pleasant to hear him converse about what is to be the future of farming in Victoria, when water has been systematically impounded, in order to flood the land in due season. Our farmers, it is to be noted, have hitherto sought the plains, where the timber was not more than was required for firewood, and where they could sow and reap at once. But the value of the forest country is now being appreciated. There is heavy clearing to be done, no doubt; but then the land is rich, and gives astonishing root crops, and fattens many sheep to the acre. And when a railway is run into the forest it is found that the timber pays for itself, and for the land also, and is as good a crop as the selector is ever likely to take off the soil.

The following are the present conditions under which land can be selected in Victoria: The best unsold portions of the public estate, amounting in the aggregate to 8,712,000 acres, are divided into 'grazing areas,' not exceeding 1000 acres in size, each of which is available for the occupation of one individual, who is entitled to select, within the limits of his block, an extent not exceeding 320 acres, for purchase in fee simple at £1 per acre, payment of which may extend over twenty years, without interest. The selected portion is termed an 'agricultural allotment,' and of it the selector is bound to cultivate one acre in every ten acres, and make other improvements amounting to a total value of at least £1 per acre. The unselected portion of the original area is intended for pastoral purposes, and for this the occupier obtains a lease, at a rental of from 2d. to 4d. per acre, for a period of fourteen years, after which it reverts to the Crown, an allowance up to 10s. per acre being made the lessee for any improvements he may have effected calculated to improve the stock-carrying capabilities of the land. In New South Wales, Queensland, and South Australia, and Western Australia, the facilities are greater than in Victoria. But it is better to state the minimum than the maximum advantage. All classes go on the lands with success, because 'high farming' or 'scientific culture' is not attempted in the bush—only in exceptional instances near the towns. A county prize for the best-kept farm was recently awarded to a freeholder whose culture and whose crops were highly commended by the judges. 'You were trained in a good school, evidently,' said one of the judges to the prize-taker. 'Not at all, sir,' was the reply; 'until I took up this land I was serving all my life behind a linen-draper's counter.' A handsome endowment has, however, just been made for the establishment of Agricultural Colleges in Australia.

Without a wife the settler's is but a lonely lot. There are bachelors, of course. Our picture represents a forlorn individual returning to his home. He will have a warmer welcome no doubt some day from wife and weans than that which he receives from the cockatoo which he has taught and tamed.

The settler has few enemies. The only two worth naming are drought and fire. The systematic storage of water throughout the country is in part mitigating the one, and already in Victoria no selector is more than three miles from permanent water for his stock. And as irrigation is coming apace, the fire risk, such as it is, will be diminished. Even now it is not serious. Not one farmer will be burned out, but at the same time a watch is required to see that no flame gets the upper hand. When a man burns off stubble he must give notice to his neighbours.

Some of the most dramatic incidents of bush life occur when an alarm of fire has been given, and the entire neighbourhood turns out to beat down the conflagration with bushes. The males form a line and work with all their energy to stamp out the flames, and the women and children help by supplying the toilers with refreshments and with a fresh stock of boughs and bushes.

'Black Thursday' (February 5, 1851), the memorable day of the colonies, would be impossible now. On that dread occasion Southern Australia was all ablaze, there was a sad loss of life, and the lurid atmosphere was noticeable as far away as New Zealand. Bishop Selwyn (who was afterwards translated to Lichfield) told the writer that he was in his yacht off the New Zealand coast at the time, and he was struck by the appearance of a fiery glow in the sky towards the island continent.

A BUSH WELCOME.

But the year 1886 unexpectedly witnessed a 'Black Thursday' on a small scale. In one corner of Victoria are situated the Cape Otway ranges, which are covered by fine forests and are the scene of a new and sparse settlement—hardy pioneers venturing in advance of the railways which they expect in due course to come up to them. The summer of 1886 opened with great heat: 100° F. was registered in the shade, and over 150° in the sun. And soon the news spread in the towns and cities of a disaster at the Otway. Steamers coming into port reported that they had passed through a pitchy darkness in the straits. One of their log records reads: 'Off Cape Otway at noon the darkness became so intense that it was necessary to light the binnacle lamp. The gloom was caused by smoke. A considerable quantity of ashes and charred sticks fell upon the deck.' This smoky volume rolled across the straits to Tasmania, and it proclaimed the fact that the forest was on fire. Fortunately to the south there is nothing behind the forest but the sea. The northerly wind, which alone fans these conflagrations, blew smoke and fire, not over parched tracts ready to burst into flame, but across the straits towards Tasmania, and the enveloped ships were not put in jeopardy, as hamlets would have been. At first it was almost forgotten that the forest was no longer lonely, but was showing here and there patches of occupation; but so it was, and a sad tale of ruin was soon told. Mr. S. H. Whittaker, who was on the heels of the flames as an '*Argus* special,' kindly supplies the following narrative: 'The night before the great fire was an anxious one in the forest. There was an ominous deep-red glow at sunset—a redness deepened by smoke rising from distant hills. The settlers, as they watched the smoke from the highest points near their selections, fervently hoped for a change of wind, for the country, scorched by the heat of midsummer, was ready to burst into a blaze. Daybreak brought with it the fierce north wind, fiery as the blast of a furnace, and strong as a gale. The bush fires could be plainly seen from many a homestead, but there was at first no apprehension of a general calamity. Some damage is done in the forest every year by fire, but never before has one hundred miles of country been left a smoking ruin. Never before have the selectors been driven half-blinded from their houses, which they had vainly sought to save, to find refuge only for their lives in their small green patches of cultivation. The settlers had seen brushwood fires, had fought the flames and conquered them after suffering some loss, and, profiting by the experience, had cleared the brushwood around their homesteads. The whole forest ablaze, the sky red with lighted fragments flying before the high wind over cleared spaces, creeks, and roads, and igniting, like the torches of a thousand incendiaries, fences, orchards, farms, crops, and buildings in many places at once, had happily never been seen before. The people vividly remember the scenes of that terrible day—how the smoke made the day blacker than night, until the flames got nearer; how these made "leaps and bounds" from tree to tree, and the terrified wallaby, dogs, cattle, fowls, and kangaroo helplessly crowded among the people, seeking shelter and protection from the common danger.

'The struggle to save the home is sometimes touchingly told. Mrs. Hurley was alone on the selection at Cowley's Creek with her seven children, her husband being away cutting grass-seed to plant in the autumn. The eldest children were a boy of fourteen and a girl of twelve. She said : " When I saw the fire coming I sent the children to the water-hole to get water in the bucket and dipper and everything that would hold it. We put the water on the fence and houses. The children all worked till they were ready to drop to save the place, even the youngest. The boy was on the roof of the house pouring water on the rafters, and the girl was on the shed. The fire came quick and scorched us. It burned in the tree branches more than on the ground. The wind blew the big sparks right at us and burned our clothes, but the little ones and myself kept going to the water-hole with the dippers and pans to keep the house wet. The boy kept the house well soaked on the roof, and I thought we might keep it safe, when one of the girls cried out, 'Mother, it's alight inside.' Then the place went all up on fire, and we couldn't get anything out. The sheds and the reaper and binder and thresher went just after, and the orchards and fences as well. The children asked me to run with them to Mrs. M'Donald, our neighbour's. I told them to run on ahead, as one of the boys had a bad foot, and I had to help him. The other children got to Mrs. M'Donald's all right, but before I could get through with the boy the forest was all burning, and the branches were coming down in showers. My boots were burnt off my feet, and I have not been able to wear a boot since. Mrs. M'Donald and the neighbours kindly helped me to put some things on the children, and Bob Cowley gave me the tent we're living in now."

'The cry, "The house is alight inside," was the despairing message from many a watcher to those who, mounted on the ridge, were striving in the blinding smoke and scorching heat to beat back the fire from the dwelling. The high wind blew live coals underneath the shingles to enkindle the canvas lining, and then the exhausted settler, foiled in his endeavour to save his or his neighbour's home, could only throw himself face downwards in his potato crop to get a breath of fresh air. But Mrs. Power, of Curdie's River, was more fortunate, and it was impossible to belie the simple and unaffected sincerity with which she devoutly ascribed her escape to the direct interposition of Providence. Her husband, like too many other selectors in the wild and inhospitable Heytesbury forest—inhospitable until by laborious toil it has been reclaimed—was away at other work when the fire happened. The holding was directly in the track of the fire. "It was on the hill yonder," said Mrs. Power, "that we were burned out seven years ago—I mean there where the scrub is as thick as ever, which shows how hard the

scrub in this forest is to kill. After we lost our first home we came to this side of the creek, and got on a little better. On the Tuesday morning the fire got all about us, in spite of my boys cutting down a tree and putting water on the fences and houses to keep them from burning. They said we had better go away; but wherever I looked there was fire; and I said, 'Where shall

BEFORE AND AFTER THE FIRE.

we go ? We might as well be burnt here, beside the old place, as anywhere else.' So I got the boys around me, and I dropped on my knees just here and prayed to the Almighty God that it should be His will to spare us, and not leave us again without a home over our heads. The clothes of one of the boys caught fire, as you see, so did the pigstye, and the eighteen bags of grass-seed that I had put in the little garden in front of the house. I expected it to go every minute, but the house stood through it all. It took fire in four places inside and out, but it did not burn, and the roof was left to cover us, in answer to my prayer. It was too hot to go into the house, and I stayed under the blackwood tree ; and the wind changed, and the drenching rain came and doused the fire. If the rain had not come, there is no knowing where the fire would have stopped."

'The rain, which will be remembered as one of the greatest downpours ever experienced in the colony, did indeed save the forest selectors from annihilation. It came just when the fire was at its height, when the trees were crashing to the ground in all directions, and when the fire, not merely scorching and singeing the bark of trees, as bush fires usually do, was consuming thousands of huge boles to charcoal, and the ground, as can still be seen, was at white heat, like a smelter's crucible. The mournfulness of the gaunt, weird scene which the fire has left is peculiarly striking and depressing. Such a mingling of night and day as the sunlight lighting the pitchy blackness of the landscape, as far as the eye can reach, is indescribably grotesque and desolate. It is hard to conceive anything like this contrast of the sunshine sparkling brightly upon the wide, inky, silent waste. It is almost like a smile upon a ghastly death's-head. There is not a bird to flutter a wing or to break the oppressive silence with a single note. There is no sign of life or what has been life, except here and there the roasted carcase of a wallaby or kangaroo. The dense forest of straight black bare boles alone reveals the might and fury of a bush fire.'

More frequent than the fire, and as thrilling, is the episode in bush life of 'the lost children.' This is a drama that is constantly enacted in the one place or the other. Australian children are quick, and they learn in a wonderful way how to travel about country, but still, where there is scrub in the neighbourhood or much undergrowth of any kind, the younger members of the family are terribly apt to go astray. The father or mother returns home to learn that 'little Johnny and the girl' were playing about, and did not come in for their evening meal. They could not have tumbled into the water-hole, for that is fenced off. They have not found their way to neighbour Dean's. There is no time to be lost. The biggest boy jumps on the colt and rides in hot haste to the nearest police-station, and rouses up neighbours on his way. The policeman telegraphs all about for aid, but faster still 'the bush telegraph' spreads the intelligence that 'Big Giles, of

Wattle Tree flat, is in trouble. Two of his little ones are astray.' Then it is that human fellowship shows to advantage. All business is laid aside. The sheep that were being bargained for are neither bought nor sold; the hay is left unstacked; the reaping is discontinued. Nothing can be done that night beyond searching around the homestead, but all night long the clatter of horses' hoofs will tell of new arrivals, and the morning will witness a couple of hundred men ready to be divided into parties and to take care that no portion of the country is unsearched.

Found!

From east and west parties will return disconsolate and silent; but the joyous 'Coo-e-e!' of the returning horsemen on the southern hill-top will tell its own tale of rescue. But rarely does a second night elapse before the distracted mother has her children with her again, and one night in the Australian bush is not likely to have injured the little ones much.

One of the most singular cases on record is that of the girl Clara Crosbie, who was lost for twenty days in the depth of winter in the Victorian uplands, where frosts will set in and where snow will fall, and who lived without food during that time. Clara was a town-bred girl, twelve years of age. Her mother took a situation in the year 1885 as housekeeper to a Lilydale farmer, some twenty-five miles away from Melbourne towards the mountains. Clara was left at a neighbour's house after she had been a few days in the district, but before she was fetched she wanted to go to her mother, and so she slipped out, got off the track easily enough, and was soon hopelessly involved in the reedy fens with which this part of the country is intersected.

A SQUATTER'S STATION.

APPENDIX.

THE RELIGIOUS STATISTICS OF THE CHIEF COLONIES.

NUMBERS are but poor tests of the religious condition and progress of a country, but they have their value, and many of the readers of this volume may find the following facts interesting. It has not been found possible to get the information respecting Queensland and Western Australia. It is quite evident at a glance that there is a large number of trained men who are engaged in the great work of the Gospel, and that their efforts are supported by a very considerable section of the Australian people.

VICTORIA.—There being no State religion in Victoria, and no money voted for any religious object, the clergy are supported by the efforts of the denomination to which they are attached. The ministers in all sections of the Church number 828, of whom 185 belong to the Church of England, 121 to the Roman Catholic Church, 177 to the Presbyterian Church, 161 to the Methodist Churches, 54 to the Independent Church, 38 to the Baptist Church, 29 to the Bible Christian Church, 56 to other Christian Churches, and 7 to the Jewish Church. Besides these there are other officials connected with these bodies, who, without being regularly ordained, perform the functions of clergymen, and are styled lay readers, lay assistants, local preachers, mission agents, &c. The number of these is not known, but it no doubt materially swells the ranks of religious instructors in the colony. The buildings used for public worship throughout Victoria number at the present time (1886) about 3700, of which 2000 are regular churches and chapels, 400 school-houses, and 1400 public or private buildings. Accommodation is provided for 500,000 persons, but the number attending the principal weekly services is said not to exceed 315,000. More than 304,000 services are performed during the year. Of the whole number of buildings used for religious worship, 764 belong to the Church of England, 618 to the Roman Catholics, 906 to the Presbyterians, 962 to the Methodists, 76 to Independents, 99 to the Baptists, 154 to the Bible Christians, 146 to other Christians, and 6 to the Jews. The Salvation Army have erected their "barracks" in various localities, and sometimes rent edifices for Divine Service, but no statistics of their operations have yet been obtained.

NEW SOUTH WALES.—With regard to religion, all the Churches stand on the same level of equality, there being no Established or State Church. These Churches are supported entirely by voluntary subscriptions, as all State aid ceased in 1862, except some small outstanding liabilities to the then existing incumbents. Roughly speaking, out of a population of 950,000 there are some 600,000 Protestants, the great majority belonging to the Church of England, and about 280,000 Roman Catholics, the remainder being made up of various denominations. At the taking of the census of 1881 the numbers were as follows; Church of England, 342,359; Lutherans, 4836; Presbyterians, 72,545; Wesleyan Methodists, 57,049; other Methodists, 7303; Congregationalists, 14,328; Baptists, 7307; Unitarians, 828; other Protestants, 9957; total Protestants, 516,512; Roman Catholics, 207,020; Catholics undescribed, 586; total Catholics, 207,606; Hebrews, 3266; other persuasions, 1042; unspecified persuasions, 13,697; Pagans, 9345. In 1883 there were 770 ministers of religion and 1521 churches, with an average attendance at public worship of 243,369 persons. The Sunday Schools have 105,162 scholars on their registers.

SOUTH AUSTRALIA.—Of this Colony the only facts obtainable are the following round numbers. The number of churches or chapels existing in 1884 was 928; the number of sittings provided was 200,123; the number of Sunday schools was 727; teachers, 6729; scholars, 57,311.

INDEX.

ABORIGINES: appearance, 167; life, 168; fighting, 168; Mr. Moore's narrative about, 169; customs, 169; dress, 170; Mr. Carr's story, 170; Ngooraialum and Bangerang tribes, 170; weapons, 173; fierceness of Northern blacks, 173; Corroboree, a, 174; cannibalism, 174; trackers, their usefulness as, 174; Mission stations, 175; Lake Tyers station, 176; Hagenauer, Rev. F. A., letter of, about, 177
Acacia, 200
ADELAIDE: founding, 103; Glenelg, 103; houses, 103, 104; streets and parks, 103; surroundings, 103; churches, 104; Victoria Square, 105; King William Street, 105; Botanical Gardens, 105
Albany, 138
Alberti, river, 125
Alligator stories, 113
Amadeus, lake, 101
Araucarias, 202
Argus snipe, 192
AUSTRALIA: former errors about, 14, 23; exports, 14; population, 14; prosperity, 14; colonies, 15; capitals, 15; people, 16; area, 19; mountains, 20; snow, 20; river system, 20; physical geography, 21; climate, 21, 76, 101, 112, 138; hot winds, 22; temperature, 22; storms, 22; natives, 23, 167, 213; fires, 23, 213; rainfall, 24; drought, losses by, 25, 76, 94, 208; not yet fully explored, 25; democracy, 29; securities, rise in, 30; federation movement, 30; immigration, 30; wages, 30; prices, 31; religion, 31; service, a rural, 32; Sunday observance, 32; sects, 34; Sunday schools, 34; church building, 34
Australia Felix, 40
Australian Alps, the, 40
Avon, river, 68

BAIRNSDALE, 69
BALLARAT: impressions, 59; Botanical Gardens, 60; discovery of gold, 60; situation, 61; the Corner, 61; Trollope on, 62
Barcoo, river, 164
Barrier Reef, the, 123
Barrow Creek, station at, 109
Bass, story of, 155
Bass's Straits, 144
Bathurst, 93
Batman, settlement of, in Victoria, 38

Baudin, M., treachery of, 157
Baxter, murder of, 158
Bear, native, 181
Beechworth, 69
Belfast, 66
Ben Lomond, 147
Bendigo, *see* SANDHURST.
Big Scrub, New South Wales, 95
Birds of Paradise, 186
Bishopscourt, view from, Melbourne, 43
Black boy, 202
Black-fish, 194
Black Spur, the, 72
Black Thursday in South Australia, 213; in Victoria, 214
Blackheath, 90
Blayney, 94
Blue gum, 200
Blue Mountains, 87
Blue wren, 186
Boomerang, the, 173
Booth, Mr. E. C., on Shepparton, 67
Boroina, 202
Bosisto, Mr. J., on Eucalyptus, 199
Botany Bay, discovery of, 76
Bottle-tree, 201
Bourke Street, Melbourne, 49
Bourke, New South Wales, 94; a winter day at, 94
Bowen, 123
Box-tree, 208
Bower bird, 188
Box-scrub, the, 136
Bream, 193
Breeza plains, 95
Bremer, river, 119
Bremoroma, 94
Brighton, a suburb of Melbourne, 43
BRISBANE, population, 119; site, 119; streets, 119; beauty, 120; garden of Acclimatisation Society, 120; houses, 121
Broome, Sir F. N., on life in Western Australia, 140
Brown, Mr. G. A., on sheep breeding, 205
Buffaloes, 113
Bulmer, Rev. J., at Lake Tyers, 176
Bundaberg, 112
Bunbury, 135
Burke, R. O'Hara, expedition of, 161
Burketown, 125
Burnett, river, 122
Bustard, 190

CAIRNS, 124
Caldwell, Mr. W. H., on the platypus, 185
Cam, river, 146

Camels at Beltana, 107
Canoona rush, the, in Queensland, 129
Cape Grant, 67,
Cape Nelson, 67
Cape Otway ranges, fire at, 214
Capertee, 91
Capitals, 15
Cardwell, 124
Carr, Mr. E. M., on the natives, 170
Carriers, 210
Castle hill, 87
Casuarina Striata, 200
Cats, native, 182
Cattle-raising, 204
Cattle, number of, in Australia, 14
Central Trunk Railway, Queensland, 122
Charters Towers, 123
Churches, the, state of, 31
Clarence, river, 96
Clermont, 123
Climate, 21, 76, 101, 112, 138
Coaching, Trollope on, 70
Cobb, who he was, 70
Cockatoo, 186
Cohan, 94
Colac lake, 65
Collins lands at Sorrento, 38
Collins Street, Melbourne, 49
Concherry, river, 162
Cook, Captain, discovers Botany Bay, 76
Cooktown, 124
Cooper's Creek, native settlement at, 164
Corangamite lake, 64
Corra Linn, 145
Corroboree, a, 174
Cotton growing in Queensland, 129
Crosbie, Clara, story of, 219
Cunningham's Gap, 119
Cutting out cattle, 204
Cycads, 202

DALBY, 122
Darling Downs, 118, 119
Darling, river, 21, 94
Dasyurido, the, 182
Deloraine, 145
Democracy, 29
D'Entrecasteaux Channel, 151
Depôt Glen, Sturt at, 23
Derwent, river, 150
Devil, Tasmanian, 182
Dibbs, Mr., on losses by drought, 25
Dingo, 183
Dog, wild, 183
Don, river, 146
Dow, Mr. T. K., on farming, 211
Drought, losses by, 25, 76, 94, 208
Dubbo, 94

INDEX.

Ducks, wild, 191; mountain duck, 191; black duck, 191; wood duck, 191; teal, 191; widgeon, 191; blue wing, 191

EAGLEHAWK NECK, 151
Elder, Sir Thomas, introduces camels, 107
Emu, chase of, 188
Emu Plains, 88; Dr. J. E. Taylor on, 90
Eucalypt, 194
Eucalyptus amygdalina, 196
E. dumosa, 199
E. ficifolia, 199
E. globus, 200
E. rostrata, 197
EXPLORATION: Sturt's exploration, 23; Bass and Flinders, story of, 155; Baudin, M., treachery of, 157; Eyre, E. J., travels of, 158; Forrest, J., journey of, 159, 164; Leichardt, L., story of, 159; Kennedy disaster, the, 160; Stuart, J. McDougall, journey of, 161; Burke's expedition, 161; M'Kinlay's party, 164; Landsborough's party, 164; Walker's party, 164; Howitt's party, 164; Warburton's party, 164
Exports of Australia, 14
Eyre, E. J., explorations of, 158
Eyre, lake, 101

FARMING, 211
FAUNA: alligators, 113; buffaloes, 113; kangaroo, 'old men,' 181, 185; marsupial mouse, 181; wombat, 181; flying fox, 181; native bear, 181; native cats, 182; Bass River opossum, 182; Tasmanian tiger-wolf, 182; Tasmanian devil, 182; dingo, 183; platypus, 185; birds, 185; parrots, 185; birds of Paradise, 185; king parrot, 186; blue mountain parrot, 186; lories, 186; parroquets, 186; love-birds, 186; blue wren, 186; cockatoos, 186; lyre-birds, 186; bower birds, 188; laughing jackass, 188; emu, 188; bustard, 190; native companion, 191; wild ducks, 191; black swan, 191; snipe, 191; quail, 192; wonga-wonga, 192; bronzewing pigeon, 192; snakes, 192; pearls, 139; shark catching, 193; trout, 193; salmon, 193; perch, 193; bream, 193; Murray cod, 193; sea salmon, 193; Murray-perch, 193; golden-perch, 193; black-fish, 194; whiting, 194; schnapper, 194
Favenc, Mr. E., on exploration, 25
Fawkner, settlement of, in Victoria, 39
Fawkner's Park, 39
Federation movement, the, 30
Feilberg, Mr. C. A., on Queensland, 117
Ferns, 196
Fig tree, the, 126
Fingal, 147
Fires, 23, 213
Fish River caves, 91
Fitzroy, river, 122
Flame-tree, 201
FLORA: nettle-tree, 127; poisonous plants, 136; box scrub, 136; rock plant, 136; heart leaf plant, 136; York road plant, 136; wild flowers,

158; eucalypt, 194; mallee scrub, 195; giant gums, 195, 197; spinifex, 195; ferns, 196; palm-tree, 196; musk-tree, 196; *Pittosporum*, 196; silver gum, 197; red gum, 197; jarrah, 136, 198; blue gum, 200; acacia or wattle, 200; tea-tree scrub, 200; shea oak, 200; bottle-tree, 201; flame-tree, 201; cycads, 202; palm lilies, 202; grass-trees, 202; warratah, 202; lomina, 202; araucarias, 202; heath, 202; grapes, 202; Mitchell grass, 205; box-tree, 208
Flinders, story of, 155
Flinders' Lane, Melbourne, 44
Flying fox, 181
Forbes, 94
Forrest, John, journey of, 159, 164
Firth, 146
Fremantle, 137

Gastrolobium acrolobiata, 136
G. bilobum, 136
G. callistachys, 136
G. calycinum, 136
Gardiner, lake, 101
GEELONG: founding, 62; growth, 62; exports, 62; tweeds of, 63
Geraldton, 135
Gippsland, scenery of, 67
Gladstone, 122
Glenelg, 103
Golden perch, 193
Golden Point, discovery of gold at, 60
Gould on Australian birds, 186
Grant, Lieut., discovers Port Phillip, 37
Grapes, 202
Grass-trees, 202
Gray, story of, 161
Great Divide, the, 96
Great West Railway, New South Wales, 87
Grey, Earl, circular of, on convicts, 135
Guildford, 135
Guilfoyle, Mr., director of the Botanic Gardens, Melbourne, 52
Gulf of Carpentaria, 125
Gums, giant, 195; height of, 196, 197
Gympie, 123; discovery of gold field at, 130

HAGENAUER, Rev. F. A., on the aborigines, 177
Harvesting system, 211
Hawkesbury sandstone, 90
Hayter, Mr. H. H., on wages, 30
Heart-leaf, the, 136
Heaths, 202
Henty, Messrs., in Portland Bay, 38
Heron, river, 151
Heytesbury forest, 215
Hindmarsh, Captain, first governor of South Australia, 103
Hobart, description of, 150
Hoddle, Robert, lays out Geelong, 62
Holdfast Bay, first landing at, 103
Horses, number of, in Australia, 14
Horsham, 67
Hospitality, 207
Hot winds, 22
Howell arrives at Port Phillip, 38
Howitt, party of, 164
Hume arrives at Port Phillip, 38

Hurleys, the, at the fire at Otway ranges, 215

IMMIGRATION, extent of, 30
Ipswich, 119, 122

JACKY, the black, fidelity of, 160
Jarrah forests, 136, 198
Jenola, 91

KANAKAS, the, 128
Kangaroo, old man, 181, 185
Kangaroo hunting, 184
Kennedy, Edmund, story of, 160
Kiama, 87
King, story of, 161
King George's Sound, 138
Kingfisher, or laughing jackass, 188
Knocklofty, 150

LAKE ST. CLAIR, 150
Lake Sorell, 150
Lake Tyers Mission Station, 176
Landells, story of, 161
Landsborough, expedition of, 164
Laughing jackass, 188
Launceston, 144
Leichardt, Ludwig, story of, 159
Leptospermum, 200
Lithgow Vale, New South Wales, 91
Livistonia palm, the 196
Loddon, river, 68
Lories, 186
Lorne, 72
Lost in the bush, 217
Louitt Bay, 72
Love-birds, 186
Lyre-bird, 186

MACARTHY, RIVER, 111
Mackay, 123
Macquarie Harbour, 151
Macquarie, river, 93
Magpie, musical, 188
Mallee scrub, rabbits in, 68; extent of, 195
Mary, river, 121
Maryborough, 121
MELBOURNE: site, 43; population, 43; area, 43; description, 43; houses, 43; Government House, 43; Exhibition Building, 43; streets, 43; Flinders' Lane, 44; Collins Street, 46; Scott's, 49; Bourke Street, 49; inrush and outrush, 49; railways, 49; public buildings, 50; university, 52; botanic gardens, 52; water supply, 52; reserves, 53; cricket, 54; the Yarra, 54; drawbacks, 55; climate, 55; unearned increment, 56
Menada, river, 145
Menura Victoriæ, the, 186
Merino sheep, 206
Mermaid's Cave, the, New South Wales, 90
Mersey, river, 145
Mitchell, Sir Thomas, verdict of, 39
Mitchell grass, 205
M'Kinlay, expedition of, 164
Moreton Bay, 118
Moore, Mr. G. F., on aborigines, 169
Morriss, Mr., school teacher to the blacks, 176
Morsman's Bay, view from, 80
Mosquito Plains, caves of the, 106

Mount Barker, 106
Mount Baw-Baw eucalypt, height of, 197
Mount Bischoff tin mine, 146
Mount Clay, 67
Mount Franklin, 40
Mount Kosciusko, 20
Mount Lindsay, 96
Mount Lofty range, 103
Mount Wellington, 130
Mountain system, 20
Mouse, marsupial, 181
Mudgee line, New South Wales, 91
Mueller, Baron von, on, tea-tree scrub, 200
Murray coal, 193
Murray perch, 193
Murray plains, 67
Murray, river, 21, 100
Musk-tree, 196
Myers, Mr. F. H., on Sydney, 79

NARRAWONG, 67
Nash discovers Gympie gold-field, 130
Native companion, the, 191
Natives, destructiveness of, 23
Nettle-tree, the, 127
New Norfolk, 150
NEW SOUTH WALES: area, 15, 75; population, 15; losses by drought, 25; climate, 76; drought, 76, 94; settlement, 76; Port Jackson, 76; statistics, 79; Sydney, 79; South Coast Railway, 84; Kiama, 87; Great West Railway, 87; Paramatta, 87; Castle Hill, 87; Toongabbie, 87; Blue Mountains, 87; Emu Plains, 88; Penrith, 89; Windsor, 89; Richmond, 89; geology, 90; Blackheath, Mermaid's Cave, 90; Lithgow Vale, 91; Capertee, 91; Mudgee line, 91; Walerawang, 91; Tarana, 91; Fish River caves, 91; Jenola, 91; Bathurst, 93; Blayney, 94; Orange, 94; Forbes, 94; Wellington Valley, 94; Dubbo, 94; cattle, 94; Darling, the, 94; Cohan, 94; Bourke, 94; Bremoruala, 94; Welcanna, 94; Wentworth, 94; Great Northern Railway, 95; Newcastle, 95; Breeza Plains, 95; Richmond, the, 95; Tweed, the, 95; Big Scrub, 95; Cane fields, 96; Great Divide, the, 96; Mount Lindsay, 96; Clarence, the, 96; Nightcap, the, 96
Newcastle, 95
Nightcap, the, New South Wales, 96
Norman, river, 125
Normanton, 125
North Esk, river, 144
Northern Territory, *see* S. Australia.
Northern Trunk Line of Queensland, 123

OAKLEIGH, a suburb of Melbourne, 43
Opossum, 182
Orange, 94
Ornithorhynchus, the, 185
Overland Telegraph Line, 108

PALM-LILIES, 202
Palm-trees, 196
Palmer gold-field, 124, 130

Palmerston, mines of, 111
Palmerston and Pine Creek line, 110
Paramatta, 87
Parrots, 185
Parroquets, 186
Peake Telegraph Station, 109
Pearl fisheries of Western Australia, 139
Penrith, 89
Perch, 193
Pérouse, expedition of, 76
Perth, description of, 136
Phillip, Captain Arthur, governor of Port Jackson, 76
Physical geography, 21
Pigeon, bronze-wing, 192
Piping crow, 188
Pittosporum, 196
Platypus, 185
Poole, death of, at Depôt Glen, 23
Population of Australia, 14
Porcupine grass, 195
Port Arthur, convicts at, 151
Port Darwin, vegetation at, 111
Port Douglas, 124
Port Essington, 113
Port Jackson, 76
PORT PHILLIP: discovery, 37; beauty, 38; Howell and Hume arrive at, 38; settlement, 38
Portland, 66
Portland Bay, 67
Potatoes, yield of, 66
Power, Mrs., at the fire at Otway ranges, 215
Prices, 31

QUAIL, 192
Quamby Bluff, 146
QUEENSLAND: area and population, 15; description, 117; settlement, 118; convicts there, 118; Toowoomba, 119, 122; Breme, the, 119; Ipswich, 119, 122; Brisbane, 119; Maryborough, 121; Rockhampton, 121; Bundaberg, 122; Gladstone, 122; Warwick, 122; Stanthorne, 122; Dalby, 122; Roma, 122; Central Trunk Railway, 122; Clermont, 123; Gympie, 123, 130; Mackay, 123; Bowen, 123; Barrier Reef, the, 123; Townsville, 123; Charters Towers, 123; Ravenswood, 123; Northern Trunk Line, 123; Cardwell, 123; Cairns, 124; Port Douglas, 124; Palmer gold field, 124, 130; Cooktown, 124; Thursday Island, 124; Gulf of Carpentaria, 125; Normanton, 125; Burketown, 125; cattle, 125; sheep farming, 125; agriculture, 126; scrublands, 126; vegetation, 126; labour question, the, 127; sugar growing, 128; exports, 128; cotton growing, 129; olives, 129; almond, 129; figs, 129; silk, 129; mineral wealth, 129; coal, 129; Canoona rush, the, 129; Nash discovers Gympie gold field, 130

RABBITS, CURSE OF, 68
Raffles Bay, 113
Railways in Victoria, 49; in Sydney, 84; in Tasmania, 152
Rainfall, 24; in Sydney, 84; in Tasmania, 152

Rainfall, taking advantage of, 209
Ravenswood, 123
Red gum, 197
Richardson, river, 68
Richmond, 89
Richmond, river, 95
Ring barking, 209
River system, 20
Rock plant, the, 136
Rockhampton, 121
Roeburne, 135
Roma, 122
Roper, river, 111; alligators in, 113
Russell, Mr. H. C., on physical geography and climate of Australia, 21

ST. HELENS, 147
St. Mary's Pass, 147
Sale, 69
Salmon, 193
Sandhurst, ups and downs of, 56; gold in, 60
Sarcophilus, the, 182
Satin bird, 188
Schools of Victoria, 70
Schnapper, 194
Scott's, Melbourne, 49
Sea-salmon, 193
Selectors, 212
Service, a rural, 32
Settler's clock, 188
Shark catching, 193
Shea-oak, 200
Sheep, number of, in Australia, 14
Sheep breeding, 205
Sheep runs, 207
Sheep shearing, 210
Shepherds, life of, 206
Shepparton, 67
Silk cultivation in Queensland, 129
Silver gum, 197
Smith, philosopher, story of, 146
Smyth, Mr. R., on native weapons, 173; on gum-trees, 197
Snakes, 192; treatment for bites of, 193
Snow, 20
Snipe, 191
Sorrento occupied by Collins, 38; beauty of, 38
SOUTH AUSTRALIA: area, 15, 99; population, 15; divisions, 99; Murray, the, 100; scenery, 100; Lake Torrens, 101; Lake Eyre, 101; Lake Gardiner, 101; Lake Amadeus, 101; climate, 101; fruits, 102; Adelaide, 103; Mount Lofty range, 103; industries, 105; wheat, 106; Mount Barker, 106; Caves of the Mosquito Plains, 106; camels at Beltana, 107; Overland Telegraph Line, 108; Peake Telegraph Station, 109; Barrow Creek 'stuck up' at, 109; railway construction, 110; Northern Territory: history, 110; settlement, 111; climate, 112; Roper, the, 111; Macarthy, the, 111; alligators, 113; buffaloes, 113; Black Thursday, 213
South Coast Railway, N. S. Wales, 84
South Esk, river, 144
South Sea Islanders in Queensland, 126
Spinifex, 195
SQUATTERS AND SETTLERS: Description, 203; cattle raising, 204; cutting out, 204; sheep breeding, 205; merino sheep, 206; hospitality,

INDEX.

207; mode of travelling, 207; sheep runs, 207; drought, 208; horses, 208; sheep shearing, 210; carriers, 210; swagmen or sundowners, 210; farming, 211; harvesting system, 211; stripper, the, 211; selecting, mode of, 212; fires, 213; lost in the bush, 217
Staghorn fern, 196
Strathorpe, 122
Stapleton, Mr., murder of, 113
Sterculia acerifolia, 201
Stevenson, falls of the, 72
Stirling, Sir James, in Western Australia, 134
Storms, 22
Strangways Springs, 110
Stripper, the, 211
Stuart, J. M. D., travels of, 110, 164
Sturt's detention at Depôt Glen, 23
Sunday observance, 32
Sundowners, 210
Surrey Hills, a suburb of Melbourne, 43
Swagmen, 210
Swan, black, 191
Swan, river, 135, 138
SYDNEY: harbour, 79; North Shore, 79; view from Morsman's Bay, 80; churches, 80; public buildings, 80; railways, 84
Sydney Cove, 76

TAMAR, river, 144
Tarana, 91
TASMANIA: a holiday resort for Australians, 143; Tamar, the, 144; Launceston, 144; North Esk, the, 144; South Esk, the, 144; Corra Linn, 145; Deloraine, 145; Menada, the, 145; Mersey, the, 145; sheep, 145; Quamby Bluff, 146; Don, the, 146; Cam, the, 146; Forth, the, 146; Mount Bischoff, 146; Waratah, the, 146; Ben Lomond, 147; St. Mary's Pass, 147; Fingal, 147; St. Helen's, 147; macadamised road, the great, 148; Hobart, 150; Derwent, the, 150; Lake St. Clair, 150; Lake Sorell, 150; New Norfolk, 150; convicts at Port Arthur, 151; Eaglehawk Neck, 151; D'Entrecasteaux Channel, 151; Heron, the, 151; Macquarie Harbour, 151; area, 151;

population, 152; revenue, 152; railways, 152; exports and imports, 152
Taylor, Dr. J. E., on Geology of Emu Plains, 90
Tea-tree scrub, 200
Temperature, 22
Tenison-Woods on the caves of the Mosquito Plains, 106
Thomas, Mr., on Lake District of Victoria, 64
Tiger-snake, 192
Tiger-wolf, Tasmanian, 182
Thursday Island, 124
Thylacinus, the, 182
Todd, Mr. Charles, and the Overland Telegraph Line, 108
Toongabbie, 87
Toowoomba, 119, 122
Torrens, lake, 101
Trackers, black, 174
Townsville, 123
Trollope, Anthony, on Ballarat, 62; on coaching, 70
Trout, 193; fly-fishing for, 194
Turkey, wild, 190
Tweed, river, 95

VICTORIA: area, 15; population, 15; protectionist, 30; foundation, 37; convicts there, 38; had name given to, 38; settlement, 38; mountains, 40; Melbourne, 43; railways, 49, 56; Sandhurst, 56; Ballarat, 59; Wendource, lake, 60; discovery of gold at Golden Point, 60; Geelong, 62; Corangamite, lake, 64; Lake Colac, 65; Warrnambool, 66; Belfast, 66; Portland, 66; potatoes, 66; Portland Bay, 67; mountains, 67; Gippsland, 67; Murray plains, 67; Shepparton, 67; Wimmera District, 67; rabbits, 68; Avon, the, 68; Richardson, the, 68; Wimmera, the, 68; Loddon, the, 68; wheat lines of railway, 68; Beechworth, 69; Sale, 69; Bairnsdale, 69; State schools, 70; Cobb, story of, 70; coaching, 70; Falls of the Stevenson, 72; Black Spur, the, 72; Louttit Bay, 72; Lorne, 72; Black Thursday, 214

WAGES, 30
Wateranwang, 91
Walker, expedition of, 164

Wallace, Mr. A. A. on flowers of Australia, 138
Waratah, river, 146
Warburton, expedition of, 164
Warratah, 202
Warwick, 122
Wattle, 200
Welcanna, 91
Wellington Valley, 94
Wendouree, lake, 60
Wentworth, 94
WESTERN AUSTRALIA: area, 15, 133; population, 15; foundation of the colony, 134; large estates in, 134; convicts, 135; Swan, river, 135; Fremantle, 135; Perth, 135; Guildford, 135; Bunbury, 135; Albany, 135; Geraldton, 135; Roebourne, 135; vegetation, 136; jarrah forests, 136; poisonous plants, 136; King George's Sound, 138; climate, 138; wild flowers of, 138; Sir F. N. Broome on life there, 140; gold discoveries, 140
Western District of Victoria, 40, 63; Mr. Thomas on, 64
Wheat lines of Wimmera, 68
Whittaker, Mr. S. H., on fire at Otway ranges, 214
Whiting, 194
Wianamatta Shale, the, 90
Wills, W. J., story of, 161
Windsor, 89
Wimmera District, 67; rabbits in, 68; wheat lines of, 68
Wimmera, river, 68
Winter day at Bourke, New South Wales, 70
Wombat, 181
Wonga-wonga, 192
Worraimbool, 66
Wreck Creek, native encampment at, 173
Wright, story of, 161
Wylie, the black boy, faithfulness of, 158

Xanthorrhœa, 202

YAGAN, an aborigine, story of, 169
Yarra Park, Melbourne, 54
Yarra, river, 54
York-road plant, the, 136

www.ingramcontent.com/pod-product-compliance
Lightning Source LLC
Chambersburg PA
CBHW031812230426
43669CB00009B/1110